Hugo's Sin

Yugoslav
Phrase Book

Hugo's Language Books Limited

Compiled by
Lexus Ltd
with
Andrijana Hewitt
and
Nada Jakir

*Facts and figures given in this book were
correct when printed. If you discover any
changes, please write to us.*

Set in 9/9 Plantin Light by
Typesetters Ltd and
printed in England by
Anchor Press Ltd

CONTENTS

PREFACE

This is the latest in a long line of Hugo Phrase Books and is of excellent pedigree, having been compiled by experts to meet the general needs of tourists and business travellers. Arranged under the usual headings of 'Hotels', 'Motoring' and so forth, the ample selection of useful words and phrases is supported by a 2,000 line mini-dictionary. By cross-reference to this, scores of additional phrases may be formed. There is also an extensive menu guide listing approximately 500 dishes or methods of cooking and presentation.

The pronunciation of words and phrases in the main text is imitated in English sound syllables, and highlighted sections illustrate some of the replies you may be given and the signs or instructions you may see or hear.

INTRODUCTION

PRONUNCIATION

When reading the imitated pronunciation, stress that part which is underlined. Pronounce each syllable as if it formed part of an English word, and you will be understood sufficiently well. Remember the points below, and your pronunciation will be even closer to the correct Serbocroat. Use our audio cassette of selected extracts from this book, and you should be word-perfect!

e: as in 'bed'.

g: always hard as in 'get'.

H: is similar to the Scottish pronunciation of 'loch'.

i: as in 'Maria' or 'Lolita'.

ī: the 'i' sound as in 'wine'.

j: as in 'jumper'.

ȷ̌:   like the 's' sound in 'leisure'.

o: as in 'hot'.

s: as in 'hiss', never as in 'his'.

y: is always as in 'yes' or 'you'.

It is very important to remember that, when the letter 'e' comes at the end of a word, this must be pronounced as a separate syllable. For example, the word 'biste' should not be said as though it were the same as the English word 'beast': it is pronounced 'bis-te'. The pronunciation guide in the phrase sections of this book adds an 'h' to a final 'e' in cases where confusion could arise.

There are two versions of Serbocroat prevalent in Yugoslavia: Serbian and Croatian. In this book we have aimed to reflect the form of Serbocroat that is known as Croatian and that is spoken in the popular tourist regions of the country, primarily along the coast.

For some common words two forms have been given. When two translations for an English word are separated by an oblique, the first translation is Croatian and the second Serbian. Both will be understood throughout Yugoslavia.

SUMMARY OF SPECIAL CHARACTERS IN SERBOCROAT

č, ć as in 'church'.

đ, dž as in 'just'.

š as in 'ship'.

ž like the 's' in 'leisure'.

USEFUL EVERYDAY PHRASES

Yes/no
Da/ne
da/ne

Thank you
Hvala
Huhvala

No thank you
Ne, hvala
ne Huhvala

Please *(offering)*
Izvolite
izvoliteh

Please *(asking for something)*
Molim
molim

I don't understand
Ne razumijem
ne razoomiyem

Do you speak English/French/German?
Govorite li engleski/francuski/njemački?
govoriteh li engleski/fran-tsooski/nyemachki

I can't speak Serbocroat
Ne govorim srpskohrvatski
ne govorim suhrpsko-Huhrvatski

USEFUL EVERYDAY PHRASES

I don't know
Ne znam
ne znam

Please speak more slowly
Molim vas govorite sporije
molim vas govoriteh sporiyeh

Please write it down for me
Molim vas napišite mi
molim vas napishiteh mi

My name is ...
Zovem se ...
zovem se

How do you do, pleased to meet you
Kako ste, drago mi je
kako ste, drago mi ye

Good morning/good afternoon/good evening
Dobro jutro/dobar dan/dobra veče
dobro yootro/dobar dan/dobra vecheh

Good night
Laku noć
lakoo noch

Goodbye
Doviđenja
dovijenya

How are you?
(polite) Kako ste; *(familiar)* kako si?
kako ste; kako si

Excuse me please
Izvinite-samo malo
izviniteh-samo malo

Sorry!
Oprostite!
oprostiteh

I'm really sorry
Jako mi je žao
yako mi je ʒa-o

Can you help me?
Možete li mi pomoći?
moʒeteh li mi pomochi

Can you tell me ...?
Možete li mi reći ...?
moʒeteh li mi rechi

Can I have ...?
Dajte mi ...?
dīteh mi

I would like ...
(said by man) Želio bih ...; *(said by woman)* željela bih ...
ʒelio biH; ʒelyela biH

Would you like ...?
Želite li ...?
ʒeliteh li

Is there ... here?
Ima li ... ovdje?
ima li ... ovd-ye

9

Where can I get ...?
Gdje mogu naći ...?
guhd-ye mogoo nachi

How much is it?
Koliko košta?
koliko koshta

What time is it?
Koliko je sati?
koliko ye sati

I must go now
Moram ići
moram ichi

I've lost my way
Izgubio sam se
izgoobio sam se

Cheers!
(to a man) Živio; *(to a woman)* živjela; *(to several people)* živjeli!
Jivio; Jivyela; Jivyeli

Do you take credit cards?
Primate li kreditne kartice?
primateh li kreditneh karti-tse

Where is the toilet?
Gdje je W.C.?
guhd-ye ye ve-tse

Excellent!
Izvrsno!
iz-vuhrsno

THINGS YOU'LL HEAR

Čuvaj se!	Look out!
Doviđenja	Goodbye
Hvala	Thanks
Hvala, dobro – a Vi?	Very well thank you – and you?
Izvolite	Here you are
Kako ste (kako si)?	How are you?
Kako ste, drago mi je	How do you do, nice to meet you
Molim	You're welcome; pardon?
Ne razumijem	I don't understand
Ne znam	I don't know
Oprostite, samo malo	Excuse me
Pazi!	Look out!
Stvarno?	Is that so?
Točno	That's right
Vidimo se kasnije	See you later

THINGS YOU'LL SEE

dizalo	lift
izlaz	way out, gate
izlaz u slučaju opasnosti	emergency exit
iznajmljuje se stan	flat for rent
kasa	till, cash point
muškarci	gentlemen
nužnik	toilet
otvoreno	open
pitka voda	drinking water
popust	reduced
posjeta	visiting hours
privatno	private
prodaje se	for sale
radno vrijeme	opening times
rasprodaja	sale
rezervirano	reserved
rini	push
sobe	rooms to let
svježa boja	wet paint
tišina	silence
toalet	toilet
ulaz	way in
ulaz slobodan	admission free
vuci	pull
zabranjeno	forbidden
zabranjen ulaz	no admittance
zahod	toilet
zatvoreno	closed
zatvoreno za vrijeme praznika	closed for holiday period
zauzeto	engaged
ženski	ladies

DAYS, MONTHS, SEASONS

Sunday	nedjelja	*ned-yel-ya*
Monday	ponedjeljak	*poned-yel-yak*
Tuesday	utorak	*ootorak*
Wednesday	srijeda	*sri-yeda*
Thursday	četvrtak	*chet-vuhr-tak*
Friday	petak	*petak*
Saturday	subota	*soobota*
January	siječanj/januar	*si-ye-chan-yuh/januar*
February	veljača/februar	*vel-yacha/februar*
March	ožujak/mart	*ojoo-yak/mart*
April	travanj/april	*travan-yuh/april*
May	svibanj/maj	*sviban-yuh/mī*
June	lipanj/juni	*lipan-yuh/yooni*
July	srpanj/juli	*suhr-pan-yuh/yooli*
August	kolovoz/august	*kolovoz/a-oogust*
September	rujan/septembar	*rooyan/septembar*
October	listopad/oktobar	*listopad/oktobar*
November	studeni/novembar	*stoodeni/novembar*
December	prosinac/decembar	*prosinats/detsembar*
Spring	proljeće	*prolyeh-che*
Summer	ljeto	*lyeto*
Autumn	jesen	*yesen*
Winter	zima	*zima*
Christmas	Božić	*bojich*
Christmas Eve	Badnjak	*badnyak*
New Year	Nova godina	*nova godina*
New Year's Eve	Stara godina	*stara godina*
Easter	Uskrs	*oos-kuhrs*
Good Friday	Veliki petak	*veliki petak*

NUMBERS

0 nula *noola*
1 jedan *yedan*
2 dva *dva*
3 tri *tri*
4 četiri *chetiri*

5 pet *pet*
6 šest *shest*
7 sedam *sedam*
8 osam *osam*
9 devet *devet*

10 deset *deset*
11 jedanaest *yedana-est*
12 dvanaest *dvana-est*
13 trinaest *trina-est*
14 četrnaest *che-tuhr-na-est*
15 petnaest *petna-est*
16 šesnaest *shesna-est*
17 sedamnaest *sedamna-est*
18 osamnaest *osamna-est*
19 devetnaest *devetna-est*
20 dvadeset *dvadeset*
21 dvadeset i jedan *dvadeset i yedan*
22 dvadeset i dva *dvadeset i dva*
30 trideset *trideset*
31 trideset i jedan *trideset i yedan*
32 trideset i dva *trideset i dva*
40 četrdeset *che-tuhr-deset*
50 pedeset *pedeset*
60 šezdeset *shezdeset*
70 sedamdeset *sedamdeset*
80 osamdeset *osamdeset*
90 devedeset *devedeset*
100 sto *sto*
110 sto deset *sto deset*
200 dvjesto *duh-vyesto*
300 tristo *tristo*
1000 tisuća/hiljada *tisoocha/hil-yada*
1,000,000 milijun/milion *mili-oon/mili-on*

TIME

today	danas	*danas*
yesterday	jučer	*yoocher*
tomorrow	sutra	*sootra*
the day before yesterday	prekjučer	*prek-yoocher*
the day after tomorrow	prekosutra	*prekosootra*
this week	ovaj tjedan	*ovī tyedan*
last week	prošli tjedan	*proshlī tyedan*
next week	slijedeći tjedan	*slīyedechi tyedan*
this morning	jutros	*yootros*
this afternoon	danas poslije podne	*danas poslīyeh podneh*
this evening	večeras	*vecheras*
tonight	noćas	*nochas*
yesterday afternoon	jučer popodne	*yoocher popodneh*
last night	jučer naveče	*yoocher navecheh*
tomorrow morning	sutra ujutro	*sootra oojootro*
tomorrow night	sutra naveče	*sootra navecheh*
in three days	za tri dana	*za tri dana*
three days ago	prije tri dana	*priyeh tri dana*
late	kasno	*kasno*
early	rano	*rano*
soon	uskoro	*ooskoro*
later on	kasnije	*kasniyeh*
at the moment	trenutno	*trenootno*
second	drugi	*droogi*
minute	minuta	*minoota*
one minute	jedna minuta	*yedna minoota*
two minutes	dvije minute	*dvi-yeh minooteh*
quarter of an hour	četvrt sata	*chet-vuhrt sata*
half an hour	pola sata	*pola sata*
three quarters of an hour	tri četvrt sata	*tri chet-vuhrt sata*

hour	sat	*sat*
that day	tog dana	*tog dana*
every day	svakog dana	*svakog dana*
all day	cijeli dan	*tsi-yeli dān*
the next day	sutradan	*sootradan*

TELLING THE TIME

To express minutes *past* the hour in Serbocroat you first say the word for the hour and then the number of minutes, using 'i' ('and') for 'past'. For example, 'dva i pet' is five past two (literally 'two and five'). For minutes *to* the hour, say the number of minutes first then the word for the hour, using 'do' for 'to'. For example, 'pet do tri' is five to three. Another way of expressing minutes to the hour is by using the word 'manje' ('minus'), so five to three is also 'tri manje pet'.

The word for 'half' is 'pola'. If placed after a figure, this becomes 'pol'. For example, half past three is 'tri i pol'. Another common way of expressing the half-hour is to put the word 'pola' in front of the *next* hour, for example 'pola četiri' (literally 'half four') means half past three. For a quarter you can say either 'petnaest' (15) or 'četvrt' (quarter). Quarter past three is therefore either 'tri i petnaest' or 'tri i četvrt'. A quarter to three is either 'petnaest do tri' or 'četvrt do tri' — or possibly 'tri manje petnaest' or 'tri manje četvrt'.

The 24-hour clock is used for timetables and often in written documents. There is no direct equivalent for a.m. and p.m. If you want to avoid ambiguity, use 'ujutro' (in the morning), 'popodne' (in the afternoon) and 'na večer' (in the evening).

a.m.	ujutro	*ooyootro*
p.m.	popodne	*popodneh*
one o'clock	jedan sat	*yedan sat*
ten past one	jedan i deset	*yedan i deset*
quarter past one	jedan i petnaest	*yedan i petna-est*
half past one	jedan i pol	*yedan i pol*
twenty to two	dvadeset do dva	*dvadeset do dva*

quarter to two	petnaest do dva	*petna-est do dva*
two o'clock	dva sata	*dva sata*
13.00	trinaest sati	*trina-est sati*
16.30	šesnaest i trideset	*shesna-est i trideset*
at half past five	u pet i pol	*oo pet i pol*
at seven o'clock	u sedam sati	*oo sedam sati*
noon	podne	*pod-ne*
midnight	ponoć	*ponoch*

HOTELS

Hotels in Yugoslavia are classified as L (de luxe), A, B, C or D, and guesthouses as 1st, 2nd and 3rd class. Many hotels offer a special all-in price to include breakfast, lunch and dinner (or breakfast with a choice of lunch or dinner) for guests staying more than three days. In recent years over 120 motels have been built along main roads and at the approaches to towns. These are marked on tourist maps by a black circle with a white M in the centre.

In many places, especially on the Adriatic, you can rent furnished apartments, villas and bungalows as well as private rooms in a family house or flat. Apartments and rooms can be booked through the tourist office in the place where you intend to stay.

Tourists are charged a visitor's tax, regardless of the kind of accommodation chosen (this includes camping sites). Hotels and tourist offices collect the tax, which varies depending on local regulations. During the low season it is usually reduced by 50%, and considerable discounts are given on all forms of accommodation.

USEFUL WORDS AND PHRASES

apartment	stan	stan
balcony	balkon	balkon
bathroom	kupaonica	koopa-onitsa
	kupatilo	koopatilo
bed	krevet	krevet
bedroom	spavaća soba	spavacha soba
bill	račun	rachoon
breakfast	doručak	doroochak
bungalow	bungalow	boongalo
dining room	blagavaonica	blagava-onitsa
dinner	večera	vechera
double room	soba s bračnim krevetom	soba suh brachnim krevetom
foyer	foaje	fo-a-ye
full board	puni pansion	pooni pansi-on

18

guesthouse	pansion	*pansi-on*
half board	polu pansion	*poloo pansi-on*
hotel	hotel	*Hotel*
key	ključ	*kuhl-yooch*
lift	lift	*lift*
lounge	salon	*salon*
lunch	ručak	*roochak*
manager	šef, direktor	*shef, direktor*
motel	motel	*motel*
reception	recepcija	*re-tsep-tsi-ya*
receptionist	recepcionist	*re-tsep-tsi-o-nist*
restaurant	restoran	*restoran*
room	soba	*soba*
room service	room service	*room servis*
shower	tuš	*toosh*
single room	jednokrevetna soba	*yedno-krevetna soba*
toilet	zahod, W.C.	*zahod, ve-tse*
twin room	dvokrevetna soba	*dvo-krevetna soba*

Have you any vacancies?
Ima li slobodnih soba?
ima li slobodniH soba

I have a reservation
Imam rezerviranu sobu
imam rezervi-ranoo soboo

I'd like a single/twin room
Molim jednu jednokrevetnu/dvokrevetnu sobu
molim yednoo yedno-krevetnoo/dvo-krevetnoo soboo

I'd like a double room
Molim sobu s bračnim krevetom
molim soboo suh brachnim krevetom

I'd like a room with a bathroom/balcony
Želio *(men)*/željela *(women)* bih sobu s kupaonicom/s balkonom
jeli-o/jelyela biH soboo suh koopa-onitsom/suh balkonom

I'd like a room for one night/three nights
Želio *(men)*/željela *(women)* bih sobu na jednu noć/tri noći
jeli-o/jelyela biH soboo na jednoo noch/tri nochi

I'd like to rent an apartment/a room in a private house
Želim iznajmiti stan/privatnu sobu
jelim iznīmiti stan/privatnoo soboo

What is the charge per night?
Koliko košta noćenje?
koliko koshta nochen-ye

I don't know yet how long I'll stay
Još ne znam koliko ću dugo ostati
yosh ne znam koliko choo doogo ostati

REPLIES YOU MAY BE GIVEN

Žao mi je, nema slobodnih soba
I'm sorry, we're full

Nema više jednokrevetnih soba
There are no single rooms left

Nema više soba s bračnim krevetom
There are no double rooms left

Koliko noći?
For how many nights?

Kako plaćate?
How will you be paying?

Molim vas platite unaprijed
Please pay in advance

When is breakfast/dinner?
U koliko je sati doručak/večera?
oo koliko je sati doroochak/vechera

Would you have my luggage brought up?
Možete li mi odnesti prtljagu u sobu?
mojeteh li mi odnesti puhrt-l-yagoo oo soboo

Please call me at ... o'clock
Molim vas probudite me u ... sati
molim vas probooditeh me oo ... sati

Can I have breakfast in my room?
Mogu li dobiti doručak u sobi?
mogoo li dobiti doroochak oo sobi

I'll be back at ... o'clock
Vraćam se u ... sati
vuhracham se oo ... sati

My room number is ...
Ja sam u sobi broj ...
ya sam oo sobi broy

I'm leaving tomorrow
Sutra odlazim
sootra odlazim

Can I have the bill please?
Račun molim?
rachoon molim

I'll pay by credit card
Plaćam kreditnom karticom
placham kreditnom kartitsom

I'll pay cash
Plaćam u gotovini
plačham oo gotovini

Can you get me a taxi?
Možete li pozvati taksi?
mojeteh li pozvati taksi

Can you recommend another hotel?
Možete li mi preporučiti neki drugi hotel?
mojeteh li mi preporoochiti neki droogi Hotel

THINGS YOU'LL SEE

dizalo	lift
doručak	breakfast
dvokrevetna soba	twin room
izlaz	exit
nužni izlaz	emergency exit
polu pansion	half board
prizemlje	ground floor
puni pansion	full board
račun	bill
recepcija	reception
restauracija	restaurant
rezervacija	reservation
rini	push
ručak	lunch
tuš	shower
vuci	pull
zahod	toilet

CAMPING AND CARAVANNING

If you want to camp in Yugoslavia you'll find a large number of official camping sites. These are very popular and can often be full, especially along the coast. No Camper's Card or any special permit is needed for official campsites. However, if you want to camp somewhere else, then you will need a special camping permit issued by the local tourist authority or 'turistički zavod' *[tooristichki zavod]*.

There is a charge for the use of camping sites which varies according to the standard of the site. In addition to this, the normal visitor's tax (see HOTELS) is charged. Food can be bought on site and there are usually restaurants nearby. At some camping sites accommodation is also available in chalets. A list of camping sites can be obtained from the Yugoslav National Tourist Office, in London and other major cities around the world.

There are also several nudist camps along the coast – marked F.K.K.

There are a few youth hostels but only in the larger towns.

USEFUL WORDS AND PHRASES

bucket	kanta	*kanta*
campfire	vatra	*vatra*
to go camping	kampirati	*kampirati*
camping permit	dozvola za kampiranje	*dozvola za kampiranyeh*
campsite	kamping	*kamping*
caravan	kamp-prikolica	*kamp-prikolitsa*
caravan site	kamping	*kamping*
chalet	bungalo	*boongalo*
cooking utensils	lonci	*lon-tsi*
drinking water	pitka voda	*pitka voda*
to hitch-hike	autostopirati	*a-ooto-stopirati*
rope	uže	*oojeh*
rubbish	smeće	*sme-che*
rucksack	ruksak	*rooksak*

saucepans	lonci	*lon-tsi*
sleeping bag	vreća za spavanje	*vrecha za spavanyeh*
tent	šator	*shator*
youth hostel	omladinski hotel	*omladinski Hotel*

Can I camp here?
Smijem li ovdje kampirati?
smiyem li ovd-ye kampirati

Can we park the caravan here?
Smijemo li ostaviti kamp-prikolicu ovdje?
smiyemo li ostaviti kamp-prikolitsoo ovd-ye

Where is the nearest campsite/caravan site?
Gdje je najbliži kamping?
guhd-ye ye nībliži kamping

Can you give me a camping permit?
Možete li mi izdati dozvolu za kampiranje?
mojeteh li mi izdati dozvoloo za kampiranyeh

What is the charge per night?
Koliko košta jedno noćenje?
koliko koshta yedno nochenyeh

Can I light a fire here?
Smijem li ložiti vatru ovdje?
smiyem li loziti vatroo ovd-ye

Where can I get ...?
Gdje mogu naći ...?
guhd-ye mogoo nachi

Is there drinking water here?
Ima li ovdje pitke vode?
ima li ovd-ye pitkeh vodeh

THINGS YOU'LL SEE OR HEAR

cijenik	charges
kamping	campsite
kamp-prikolica	caravan
kuhinja	kitchen
omladinski hotel	youth hostel
osobna karta	identity card
pitka voda	drinking water
prikolica	trailer
propusnica	pass
svjetlo	light
šator	tent
toalet	toilet
tuš	shower
vreća za spavanje	sleeping bag
zabranjeno kampiranje	no camping
zahod	toilet

MOTORING

You can drive into Yugoslavia from seven countries – Italy, Austria, Hungary, Rumania, Bulgaria, Greece and Albania. The frontiers are open 24 hours a day. No customs documents are required for private cars and motorcycles, but you must have a green insurance card (you can buy insurance at the border, should this prove necessary). Although a national driving licence is usually acceptable, since the British driving licence has no photograph in it you should carry an international driving licence. This will make life simpler should you ever be stopped by the police.

The Yugoslav road network has been greatly improved in recent years and there are quite long stretches of motorway, mainly linking the larger towns. In more remote areas, however, you are still likely to come across badly worn roads and dirt tracks.

Traffic signs in Yugoslavia are the same as those generally recognized in the rest of Europe, as are the rules of the road. Drive on the right, overtake on the left. The maximum speed limit on motorways is 120 kph (75 mph), and on major roads it is 100 kph (62 mph). On all other roads it is 80 kph (50 mph), with a limit of 60 kph (37.5 mph) applying in built-up areas. Equipment to be carried at all times includes a spare set of bulbs and a red triangle in case of an accident or breakdown. The wearing of seat belts is compulsory.

There is no shortage of petrol stations in the towns and along major roads, and many of them are open 24 hours. There are two fuel ratings: normal (86 octane) and super (98 octane). Foreign motorists visiting Yugoslavia may purchase petrol coupons at the border. These coupons give a discount on normal petrol prices but must be paid for in convertible currency, i.e. in sterling, dollars, German marks or French francs etc and not in Yugoslavian dinars.

SOME COMMON ROAD SIGNS

automehaničarska radnja	garage
autoput (cestarina)	motorway (with toll)
benzin	petrol
benzinska stanica	service station
carina	customs
centar grada	town centre
cestarina	toll
čvor	interchange (motorway)
garaža	garage
kraj autoputa	end of motorway
neravni kolnik	bad surface
ograničeno parkiranje	restricted parking (zone)
opasan zavoj	dangerous bend
opasno	danger
osim bus	buses only
osim dostave	deliveries only
parking	car park
parkiranje zabranjeno	no parking
pažnja	caution, watch out
pješaci	pedestrians
pješaci držite se lijevo	pedestrians keep to the left
pješačka zona	pedestrian precinct
podvožnjak	subway
pretjecanje zabranjeno	no overtaking
prva pomoć	first-aid
radovi na putu	roadworks
rampa	level crossing
raskršće	crossroads
stalno u upotrebi	in constant use
škola	school
ugasite svjetla	headlights off

→

ulaz zabranjen	no entry
upali svjetla	headlights on
upozorenje	watch out
uspori	slow
vozi oprezno	drive carefully
zabranjen prilaz	no trespassing
zaobilazak	diversion
za teretna vozila	for heavy vehicles

USEFUL WORDS AND PHRASES

automatic	automatski	*a-ootomatski*
boot	prtljažnik	*puhrt-lyaȳ-nik*
brake	kočnica	*kochnitsa*
breakdown	kvar	*kuh-var*
car	auto, kola	*a-ooto, kola*
caravan	kamp prikolica	*kamp-prikolitsa*
clutch	kvačilo, kuplung	*kuh-vachilo, kooploong*
crossroads	raskršće	*ras-kuhrsh-che*
to drive	voziti	*voziti*
engine	motor	*motor*
exhaust	auspuh	*a-oospooH*
fanbelt	remen	*remen*
garage *(repairs)*	automehaničarska radnja	*a-ooto-meHanicharska radn-ya*
(petrol)	benzinska stanica	*benzinska stanitsa*
gear	zupčanik	*zoop-chanik*
gears	zupčanici	*zoop-chanitsi*
green card	zeleni karton	*zeleni karton*
junction *(motorway)*	križanje	*kriȳan-ye*
licence	dozvola	*dozvola*

lights *(head)*	farovi	*farovi*
(rear)	poziciona svjetla	*pozitsi-ona svyetla*
lorry	kamion	*kami-on*
manual	ručno	*roochno*
mirror	retrovizor	*retrovizor*
motorbike	motocikl	*moto-tsikuhl*
motorway	autoput	*a-ootopoot*
number plate	registarska tablica	*registarska tablitsa*
petrol	benzin	*benzin*
petrol coupon	kuponi za benzin	*kooponi za benzin*
road	cesta	*tsesta*
to skid	skliznuti	*skliznooti*
spares	rezervni djelovi	*rezervni duh-yelovi*
speed	brzina	*buhr-zina*
speed limit	ograničenje brzine	*ogranichen-ye buhr-zineh*
speedometer	brzinomjer	*buhr-zino-myer*
steering wheel	volan	*volan*
to tow	vući	*voochi*
traffic lights	semafori	*semafori*
trailer	prikolica	*prikolitsa*
tyre	guma	*gooma*
van	kombi	*kombi*
wheel	točak	*tochak*
windscreen	prednje staklo, šajba	*predn-ye staklo, shi-ba*
wipers	brisači	*brisachi*

I'd like some petrol/oil/water
Molim vas benzina/ulja/vode
molim vas benzina/ool-ya/vodeh

Fill her up please!
Napunite molim!
napooniteh molim

I'd like 10 litres of petrol
Deset litara benzina molim
deset litara benzina molim

Would you check the tyres please?
Možete li pogledati gume molim vas?
moʒeteh li pogledati goomeh molim vas

Where is the nearest garage?
Gdje je najbliža garaža?
guhd-ye ye nī-bliʒa garaʒa

How do I get to ...?
Kako doći do ...?
kako dochi do

Is this the road to ...?
Da li ye ovo cesta za ...?
da li ye ovo tsesta za

DIRECTIONS YOU MAY BE GIVEN

ravno	straight on
na lijevo	on the left
okrenite na lijevo	turn left
na desno	on the right
okrenite na desno	turn right
prva desno	first on the right
druga lijevo	second on the left
nakon ...	past the ...

Do you do repairs?
Da li radite popravke?
da li raditeh popravkeh

Can you repair the clutch?
Možete li popraviti kvačilo?
mojeteh li popraviti kuh-vachilo

How long will it take?
Koliko će dugo trajati?
koliko che doogo tra-yati

There's something wrong with the engine
Nešto nije u redu s motorom
neshto ni-ye oo redoo suh motorom

The engine is overheating
Motor se pregrijava
motor se pregri-yava

The brakes are binding
Kočnice se uglavljuju
kochnitseh se ooglav-lyoo-yoo

I need a new tyre
Treba mi nova guma
treba mi nova gooma

Where can I park?
Gdje mogu parkirati?
guhd-ye mogoo parkirati

Can I park here?
Mogu li ovdje parkirati?
mogoo li ovd-ye parkirati

I'd like to hire a car
Želio *(men)*/željela *(women)* bih iznajmiti auto
jeli-o/jelyela biH iznīmiti a-ooto

31

Is there a mileage charge?
Da li se posebno računa kilometraža?
da li se posebno rachoona kilometraja

THINGS YOU'LL SEE OR HEAR

autoput	motorway
autoput s cestarinom	motorway with toll
benzin	petrol
benzinska stanica	petrol station
brisać	windscreen wiper
izlaz	exit
mješavina	diesel
normal	2 star
popravak	repair
pritisak zraka	air pressure
pritisak zraka u gumama	tyre pressure
raskršće na autoputu	motorway junction
razina ulja	oil level
spori kolosjek	crawler lane
super	4 star
ulje	oil
zaobilaznica	diversion

Želite li automatik ili ručna kola?
Would you like an automatic or a manual?

Molim vašu vozačku dozvolu?
May I see your licence?

RAIL & LONG-DISTANCE COACH TRAVEL

Yugoslav trains are quite fast and the fares are very cheap compared with the rest of Europe. For longer journeys couchettes and sleeping cars are available, but these have to be booked in advance. The trains running across the country and down to the coastal resorts are often very full, so advance booking is again recommended. Between major cities there are a number of very fast 'business trains' or 'poslovni vlak' which are first-class only; these usually leave very early in the morning and return in the evening. The Arena Express runs between Pula and Zagreb; the Marjan Express runs between Split and Zagreb.

There is a good coach service covering the whole of the country, with coaches leaving at frequent intervals. Coach travel is even cheaper than by rail and advance booking is recommended. Coaches leave from the main coach station in town, the 'autobusni kolodvor'. There are no refreshments available on the coaches but they do make fairly frequent stops, allowing time for passengers to get a meal or a snack.

USEFUL WORDS AND PHRASES

booking office	prodaja karata	_prodīa karata_
buffet	buffet	_bifeh_
bus, coach	autobus	_a-ootoboos_
carriage	vagon	_vagon_
compartment	kupe	_koopeh_
connection	veza	_veza_
couchette	couchette	_kooshet_
dining car	restoran kola	_restoran kola_
emergency brake	kočnica za slučaj opasnosti	_kochnī-tsa za sloochī opasnosti_
engine	motor	_motor_
entrance	ulaz	_oolaz_
exit	izlaz	_īzlaz_
first class	prvi razred	_puhr-vi razred_

33

to get in	ući	*oochi*
to get out	sići	*sichi*
guard	skretničar	*skretnichar*
left luggage	garderoba	*garderoba*
lost property	izgubljeno-nađeno	*izgoob-lyeno-najeno*
luggage rack	polica za prtljagu	*politsa za puhrt-lyagoo*
luggage trolley	kolica za prtljagu	*kolitsa za puhrt-lyagoo*
luggage van	teretni vagon	*teretni vagon*
platform	peron	*peron*
rail	pruga	*prooga*
railway	željeznica	*je-lyez-nitsa*
reserved seat	rezervacija	*rezervatsi-ya*
restaurant car	restoran kola	*restoran kola*
return ticket	povratna karta	*povratna karta*
seat	sjedište	*suh-yedishteh*
second class	drugi razred	*droogi razred*
single ticket	karta u jednom smjeru	*karta oo yednom suh-myeroo*
sleeping car	spavaća kola	*spavacha kola*
station	kolodvor/stanica	*kolodvor/stanitsa*
station master	šef stanice	*shef stanitseh*
ticket	karta	*karta*
ticket collector	kondukter	*kondookter*
timetable	vozni red	*vozni red*
tracks	tračnice	*trachnitseh*
train	vlak/voz	*vuh-lak/voz*
waiting room	čekaonica	*cheka-onitsa*
window	prozor	*prozor*

When does the train for ... leave?
Kada polazi vlak za ...?
kada polazi vuh-lak za

When does the train from ... arrive?
Kada stiže vlak iz ...?
kada stijeh vuh-lak iz

When is the next train to ...?
Kada je slijedeći vlak za ...?
kada ye sliyedechi vuh-lak za

When is the first train to ...?
Kada je prvi vlak za ...?
kada ye puhr-vi vuh-lak za

When is the last train to ...?
Kada je posljednji vlak za ...?
kada ye poslyednyi vuh-lak za

What is the fare to ...?
Koliko dođe karta za ...?
koliko dojeh karta za

Do I have to change?
Moram li presjedati?
moram li presyedati

Does the train stop at ...?
Da li vlak stoji kod ...?
da li vuh-lak stoyi kod

How long does it take to get to ...?
Koliko treba do ...?
koliko treba do

A single ticket to ... please
Običnu kartu za ... molim
obichnoo kartoo za ... molim

A return ticket to ... please
Povratnu kartu za ... molim
povratnoo kartoo za ... molim

Do I have to pay a supplement?
Da li moram nadoplatiti?
da li moram nadoplatiti

I'd like to reserve a seat
Želio *(men)*/željela *(women)* bih rezervirati mjesto
želi-o/želyela biH rezervirati myesto

Is this the right train for ...?
Da li je ovo vlak za ...?
da li ye ovo vuh-lak za

Is this the right platform for the ... train?
Da li vlak za ... dolazi na ovaj peron?
da li vuh-lak za ... dolazi na ovī peron

Which platform for the ... train?
S kog perona ide vlak za ...?
suh kog perona ideh vuh-lak za

Is the train late?
Da li vlak kasni?
da li vuh-lak kasni

Could you help me with my luggage please?
Možete li mi pomoći s prtljagom molim?
možeteh li mi pomochi suh puhrt-lyagom molim

Is this a non-smoking compartment?
Da li je zabranjeno pušenje u ovom kupeu?
da li ye zabran-yeno pooshenyeh oo ovom koopeh-oo

Is this seat free?
Da li je slobodno ovo mjesto?
da li ye slobodno ovo myesto

This seat is taken
Ovo je mjesto zauzeto
ovo ye myesto za-oozeto

I have reserved this seat
Imam rezervaciju za ovo mjesto
imam rezervatsi-oo za ovo myesto

May I open the window?
Smijem li otvoriti prozor?
smiyem li otvoriti prozor

May I close the window?
Smijem li zatvoriti prozor?
smiyem li zatvoriti prozor

When do we arrive in ...?
Kada stižemo u ...?
kada stiʒemo oo

What station is this?
Koja je ovo stanica?
koya ye ovo stanitsa

Do we stop at ...?
Da li vlak stoji kod ...?
da li vuh-lak stoyi kod

Would you keep an eye on my things for a moment?
Možete li mi pričuvati stvari na trenutak?
moʒeteh li mi prichoovati stvari na trenootak

Is there a restaurant car on this train?
Da li ovaj vlak ima restoran kola?
da li ovay vuh-lak ima restoran kola

THINGS YOU'LL SEE OR HEAR

čekaonica	waiting room
dolasci	arrivals
garderoba	left luggage
glavni kolodvor	central station
hvala što ne pušite	thank you for not smoking
informacije	information
JŽ	Yugoslavian National Railways
izlaz	exit
kiosk	newspaper kiosk
kočnica za slučaj opasnosti	emergency brake
lokalni vlak	local train
mjenjačnica	currency exchange
nadoplata	supplement
nedjeljom i praznicima	Sundays and public holidays
ne naginji se kroz prozor	do not lean out of the window
ne stoji kod ...	does not stop in ...
odlasci	departures
osim nedjeljom	Sundays excepted
peron	platform
poslovni vlak	business train, fast Intercity
prodaja karata	tickets, ticket office
pušači	smokers
pušenje zabranjeno	no smoking
put, putovanje	journey
rezervacija	seat reservation
samo radnim danom	weekdays only
slobodno	vacant
spavača kola	sleeping car
ulaz	entrance
ulaz zabranjen	no entry
vagon	carriage
vlakovi	to the trains
vozni red	timetable

→

zabranjeno hodanje prugom	do not walk on the railway lines
zauzeto	engaged
zloupotreba se kažnjava	penalty for misuse

Pažnja
Attention

Molim vas vašu kartu
Tickets please

AIR TRAVEL

Yugoslav Airlines (JAT) and Adria Airways operate international flights to many parts of the world. The domestic network is also very good, although it can be difficult to fly between the coastal resorts. Sometimes you have to fly inland to Zagreb or Belgrade and then take another flight to the coastal town you are heading for.

USEFUL WORDS AND PHRASES

aircraft	avion	*avi-on*
air hostess	stjuardesa	*styoo-ardesa*
airline	avionska kompanija	*avi-onska kompaniya*
airport	aerodrom	*a-erodrom*
airport bus	aerodromski autobus	*a-erodromski a-ootoboos*
aisle	prolaz	*prolaz*
arrival	dolazak	*dolazak*
baggage claim	prtljaga	*puhrt-lyaga*
boarding card	karton za ulaz u avion, 'boarding card'	*karton za oolaz oo avi-on, bording kard*
check-in desk	'check-in', registracija putnika	*chek-in, registratsi-ya pootnika*
customs	carina	*tsarina*
delay	kašnjenje	*kash-nye-nye*
departure	odlazak	*odlazak*
departure lounge	predvorje za odlazak	*predvoryeh za odlazak*
domestic arrivals	domaći dolazak	*domachi dolazak*
domestic departures	domaći odlazak	*domachi odlazak*
duty free	bescarinska prodaja	*bes-tsarinska prodia*
emergency exit	izlaz u slučaju opasnosti	*izlaz oo sloochioo opasnosti*
flight	let	*let*
flight number	broj leta	*broy leta*
gate	izlaz	*izlaz*

international arrivals	međunarodni dolazak	*mejoonarodnee dolazak*
jet	mlazni avion	*mlazni avi-on*
to land	sletjeti	*slet-yeti*
long distance flight	prekooceanski let	*preko-otseh-anski let*
passport	pasoš	*pasosh*
passport control	pasoška kontrola	*pasoshka kontrola*
pilot	pilot	*pilot*
runway	pista	*pista*
seat	sjedište	*suh-yedishteh*
seat belt	sigurnosni pojas	*sigoornosni poyas*
steward	stjuard	*styoo-ard*
stewardess	stjuardesa	*styoo-ardesa*
take-off	uzlijetanje	*uzliyetan-ye*
window	prozor	*prozor*
wing	krilo	*krilo*

When is there a flight to ...?
Kada ima avion za ...?
kada ima avi-on za

What time does the flight to ... leave?
Kada odlazi avion za ...?
kada odlazi avi-on za

Is it a direct flight?
Da li leti direktno?
da li leti direktno

Do I have to change planes?
Da li je potrebno presjedati?
da li ye potrebno pres-yedati

When do I have to check in?
kada moram čekirati?
kada moram chekirati

AIR TRAVEL

I'd like a single ticket to ...
Jednosmjernu kartu za ... molim
yedno-suhmyernoo kartoo za ... molim

I'd like a return ticket to ...
Povratnu kartu za ... molim
povratnoo kartoo za ... molim

I'd like a non-smoking seat please
Nepušačko mjesto molim
nepooshachko myesto molim

I'd like a window seat please
Molim vas sjedište pokraj prozora
molim vas syedishteh pokrī prozora

How long will the flight be delayed?
Koliko kasni avion?
koliko kasni avi-on

Is this the right gate for ...?
Da li je ovo izlaz za ...?
da li ye ovo izlaz za

Which gate for the flight to ...?
Koji je izlaz za let za ...?
koyi ye izlaz za let za

When do we arrive in ...?
Kada stižemo u ...?
kada stižemo oo

May I smoke now?
Smijem li sada pušiti?
smiyem li sada pooshiti

I do not feel very well
Ne osjećam se dobro
ne osyecham se dobro

THINGS YOU'LL SEE OR HEAR

avion	aircraft
carinska kontrola	customs control
čekirati	to check-in
direktan let	direct flight
dolasci	arrivals
domaći	domestic
informacije	information
izlaz	exit, gate
kasni	delayed
let	flight
međunarodni	international
nepušači	non-smokers
nužni izlaz	emergency exit
odlasci	departures
pasoška kontrola	passport control
prodaja karata	ticketing
prtljaga	baggage claim
putnici	passengers
redovni let	scheduled flight
registracija putnika	check-in
vežite sigurnosne pojaseve	fasten seat belts
zabranjeno pušenje	no smoking please

Molim vas uputite se na izlaz broj ...
Please go now to gate number ...

43

LOCAL TRANSPORT, BUS & BOAT

The major Yugoslav cities have a good bus network – and some cities have trams. Buses and trams are one-man operated and you pay a flat-rate fare as you enter. It is also possible to buy a book of 10 tickets called a 'karnet'; when you board the vehicle you have to punch your ticket in a punching machine.

Taxis usually wait at taxi ranks; you will rarely be able to flag one down in the street. Taxi fares are reasonable but 20% is added after 10.00 p.m., and on Sundays and bank holidays. Check that the driver has turned the taximeter on as you set off. It is not unusual, especially in remoter parts of the country, to use taxis for quite long journeys. But make sure that you agree the price with the driver first.

Ferry boat services operate all along the Adriatic coast, linking the coastal towns and carrying cars and passengers to the numerous islands. They also cross the Adriatic to Italian ports. The ferries are in great demand and it is a good idea to join the queue early. Using the ferries can make good sense if you are driving – the ferry across the Bay of Kotor, for example, takes 15 minutes and saves a long 50 kilometre drive on winding roads all around the bay. There are also hydrofoils which will whisk you over the waves to your holiday island, much faster than the ferries.

USEFUL WORDS AND PHRASES

adults	odrasli	*odrasli*
boat	brod	*brod*
bus	autobus	*a-ootoboos*
bus station	autobusni kolodvor/ autobuska stanica	*a-ootoboosni kolodvor/ a-ootobooska stanitsa*
bus stop	autobusno stajalište	*a-ootoboosno stī-alishteh*
child	dijete	*di-yeteh*
coach	autobus	*a-ootoboos*
conductor	kondukter	*kondookter*

connection	veza	*veza*
cruise	krstarenje	*kuhrs-tarenyeh*
driver	vozač	*vozach*
fare	vozarina, karta	*vozarina, karta*
ferry	trajekt	*tra-yekt*
lake	jezero	*yezero*
network map	karta	*karta*
number 5 bus	autobus broj pet	*a-ootoboos broy pet*
passenger	putnik	*pootnik*
port	luka	*looka*
quay	kej	*kay*
river	rijeka	*ri-yeka*
sea	more	*moreh*
seat	sjedište, mjesto	*suh-yedishte, myesto*
ship	brod	*brod*
station	kolodvor/stanica	*kolodvor/stanitsa*
subway	podvožnjak	*pod-voj-nyak*
taxi	taksi	*taksi*
terminus	terminal	*terminal*
ticket	karta	*karta*
tram	tramvaj	*tram-vī*

Where is the bus station?
Gdje je autobusni kolodvor?
guhd-ye ye a-ootoboosni kolodvor

Where is there a bus stop?
Gdje je autobusno stajalište?
guhd-ye ye a-ootoboosno stī-alishteh

Which buses go to ...?
Koji autobus ide do ...?
koyi a-ootoboos ideh do

How often do the buses/ferries to ... run?
Kako često ide autobus/trajekt za ...?
kako chesto ideh a-ootoboos/tra-yekt za

Would you tell me when we get to ...?
Možete li mi reći kad stignemo u ...?
mojeteh li mi rechi kad stignemo oo

Do I have to get off yet?
Da li još treba sići?
da li yosh treba sichi

How do you get to ...?
Kako se dođe do ...?
kako se dojeh do

Is it very far?
Da li je daleko?
da li ye daleko

I want to go to ...
Želim ići u ...
jelim ichi oo

Do you go near ...?
Da li idete blizu ...?
da li ideteh blizoo

Where can I buy a ticket?
Gdje mogu kupiti kartu?
guhd-ye mogoo koopiti kartoo

Could you open/close the window?
Da li biste mogli otvoriti/zatvoriti prozor?
da li bisteh mogli otvoriti/zatvoriti prozor

46

Could you help me get a ticket?
Da li biste mi mogli pomoći kupiti kartu?
da li bisteh mi mogli pomochi koopiti kartoo

When does the last bus/ferry leave?
Kada ide posljednji autobus/trajekt?
kada ideh pos-lyed-nyi a-ootoboos/tra-yekt

Which island is this?
Koji je ovo otok?
koyi ye ovo otok

How much will you charge to take me to ...?
Koliko bi došla vožnja do ...?
koliko bi doshla vojnya do

Will you wait here and take me back?
Možete li me pričekati ovdje pa me povesti natrag?
mojete li me prichekati ovd-ye pa me povesti natrag

THINGS YOU'LL SEE

autobusni kolodvor	coach station
blagajna	ticket office
djeca	children
izlaz	exit
izlaz u slučaju opasnosti	emergency exit
karnet	book of 10 bus tickets
karta	ticket
luka	harbour
ne ometaj vozača u vožnji	do not disturb the driver
odlazak	departure
odrasli	adults
pušenje zabranjeno	no smoking
sjedišta	seats
stajalište autobusa	bus stop
stajalište tramwaya	tram stop
taksi stajalište	taxi rank
terminal	terminus
ulaz	entrance
ulaz naprijed/otraga	entry at the front/rear
ulaz zabranjen	no entry
vozač	driver

RESTAURANTS

Yugoslavs like their food and there is a large selection of regional dishes for the adventurous to try out. The large hotels tend to cater for their international clientele with rather neutral 'international' menus, but if you venture out to the small local restaurants, you will find a wonderful choice of regional dishes.

There is the 'riblji restoran' *[riblyi restoran]* or seafood restaurant – the dishes simply prepared to great effect with a garnish of olive oil, parsley and garlic or tomato sauce, and served with boiled potatoes and a salad. This is the cuisine of the people of the Adriatic coast.

You will also find restaurants specializing in spit-roast lamb and sucking pig – ordered by the kilo and served with nothing more than a plateful of chopped onion and mounds of freshly baked bread. These restaurants are usually situated just outside town and will display a sign advertising the spit-roast lamb and sucking pig. Look for 'janjetina i odojak na ražnju' *[yan-yetina i odoyak na rajnyoo]*.

Each region of Yugoslavia has its own local cuisine and should you find yourself in the Zagreb area (capital of Croatia) try the 'pura s mlincima' *[poora suh mlin-tsima]* – roast turkey with a special pastry to soak up the meat juices – or the 'štruklji' *[shtrooklyi]* – a special pastry, sweet or savoury, boiled like dumplings filled with curd cheese and served with sour cream.

Self-service restaurants or 'samoposluga' *[samoposlooga]* offer a good selection of local dishes. Try 'grah varivo' *[graH varivo]*, the kind of thing people eat at home – thick bean soups with or without sausages, chunks of boiled bacon and/or a pork chop or two. Or the 'sarma' and 'punjene paprike' *[poonyeneh paprikeh]* – cabbage leaves and green peppers stuffed with minced meat etc.

There are also numerous small restaurants called 'ćevabdžinica' *[chevab-jini-tsa]* serving 'ćevapčići' *[chevapchichi]* and 'ražnjići' *[rajnyichi]* – small sausage shapes of minced meat, and pork kebabs respectively, grilled on charcoal, and served with pitta bread or 'lepinja' *[lepinya]*.

You could go to a 'gostionica' *[gosti-onitsa]* which is a kind of inn, serving just drinks and perhaps sandwiches or else to a 'buregdžija' *[booreg-jiya]*, a small restaurant or kiosk selling 'burek' *[boorek]* – flaky pastry pies with meat or cheese filling. A special treat is a visit to the 'slastičarna' *[slasticharna]* where you will find a large variety of cakes, ice cream and soft drinks.

Last but not least, try the 'kavana' *[kavana]* or coffee house and the small coffee bars or 'kafe-bar', where you can spend hours sipping a drink and chatting to friends.

USEFUL WORDS AND PHRASES

beer	pivo	*pivo*
bill	račun	*rachoon*
bottle	boca/flaša	*botsa/flasha*
bowl	zdjela	*zuh-dyela*
cake	kolač	*kolach*
chef	kuhar	*koohar*
coffee	kava	*kava*
cup	šalica	*shalitsa*
fork	viljuška	*vil-yooshka*
glass	čaša	*chasha*
knife	nož	*noj*
menu	jelovnik	*yelovnik*
milk	mlijeko	*muh-liyeko*
plate	tanjur	*tan-yoor*
receipt	račun	*rachoon*
sandwich	sendvič	*sendvich*
serviette	salveta	*salveta*
snack	nešto za prezalogajiti	*neshto za prezalogi-iti*
soup	juha	*yooha*
spoon	žlica	*juh-litsa*
sugar	šećer	*shecher*
table	stol	*stol*
tea	čaj	*chi*
teaspoon	žličica	*juh-lichitsa*

tip	napojnica	*napoynitsa*
waiter	konobar	*konobar*
waitress	konobarica	*konobaritsa*
water	voda	*voda*
wine	vino	*vino*
wine list	cjenik pića	*tsyenik picha*

A table for one please

Molim vas stol za jednu osobu
molim vas stol za yednoo osoboo

A table for two please

Molim vas stol za dvije osobe
molim vas stol za duh-viyeh osobeh

Can I see the menu?

Dajte mi jelovnik, molim vas?
diteh mi yelovnik molim vas

Can I see the wine list?

Dajte mi cjenik pića, molim vas?
diteh mi tsyenik picha molim vas

What would you recommend?

Što biste mi preporučili?
shto bisteh mi preporoochili

I'd like ...

Želio *(men)*/željela *(women)* bih ...
jeli-o/jelyela biH

Just a cup of coffee, please

Samo kavu, molim
samo kavoo molim

Waiter/Waitress!
Konobar!/konobarice!
konobar/konobaritseh

Can we have the bill, please?
Račun, molim
rachoon molim

I only want a snack
Samo ću nešto malo prezalogajiti
samo choo neshto malo prezalogī-iti

I didn't order this
Ovo nisam naručio *(men)*/naručila *(women)*
ovo nisam naroochi-o/naroochila

May we have some more ...?
Možemo li dobiti još ...?
možemo li dobiti yosh

The meal was very good, thank you
Bilo je vrlo ukusno, hvala
bilo je vuhr-lo ookoosno Huh-vala

My compliments to the chef!
Komplimenti šefu kuhinje
komplimenti shefoo koohin-ye

YOU MAY HEAR

Prijatno/Dobar tek
Enjoy your meal

MENU GUIDE

ajvar	relish made of aubergine and peppers
ananas	pineapple
bademi	almonds
baklava	rich cake in syrup made of thin layers of pastry filled with walnuts
barbun	red mullet
batak	leg (poultry)
bećki odrezak	Wiener schnitzel
beefsteak na tatarski	steak tartar
bešamel umak	sauce béchamel
bijela kava	white coffee
bijeli bubrezi	sweetbreads
bijeli kruh	white bread
bijeli luk	garlic
bijelo meso	breast (poultry)
bijelo vino	white wine
blitva	mangold
borovnice	blackcurrants
bosanski lonac	Bosnian hot-pot
brašno	flour
brendi	brandy
breskve	peaches
brodet na dalmatinski način	bouillabaisse Dalmatian style (fish stew)
bubrezi	kidneys
burek	minced meat or cheese in flaky pastry pie
but	leg
celer	celery root
cikorija	chicory
cipal	grey mullet
Colbert juha	broth with an egg yolk floating on it
crna kava	black coffee
crni kruh	brown bread
crno vino	red wine
čaj	tea
čaj sa limunom	tea with lemon
češnjak	garlic

čorba	(thick) soup
čorba od goveđeg repa	oxtail soup
čorbast pasulj sa kobasicama	bean stew with sausages
ćevapčići	rolls minced meat
ćufte na luku	meatballs with onions
ćufte u sosu od rajčica	meatballs in tomato sauce
ćulbastija	grilled cut of well-matured beef best rib
dagnje	mussels
dimljeni bakalar	smoked cod
dimljeni sir	smoked cheese
dinja	melon
divljač	game
dobro pečen	well done
domaće kobasice na žaru	grilled home-made sausages
dunja	quince
džem	jam
džem od bresaka	peach jam
džem od jagoda	strawberry jam
džem od kajsija	apricot jam
džem od marelica	apricot jam
džem od šipaka	rose hip jam
džem od šljiva	plum jam
džigerica na žaru	grilled liver
džin	gin
đuveč	dish made of meat, rice and various vegetables
faširane šnicle	minced meat steaks
feferoni	chillies
francuska salata	French salad – mixed vegetables and ham in mayonnaise
gibanica	layered cheese pie
girica	type of small pike
gljive	mushrooms
govedina	beef
govedina sa hrenom	cold beef with horseradish
goveđa juha	beef soup
goveđa juha sa rezancima	beef soup with noodles
goveđe pečenje	roast beef
goveđi gulaš	beef goulash

goveđi jezik	ox tongue
goveđi odrezak sa lukom	beef steak with onion
govedska juha s domaćim rezancima	beef soup with home-made noodles
grah	beans
grašak	peas
grejpfrut	grapefruit
grožđe	grapes
grožđice	raisins
hladna zakuska	mixed hors d'oeuvre
hren	horseradish
hrenovke	frankfurters; hot-dogs
integralna riža	brown rice
istarski brodet	Istrian bouillabaisse (fish stew)
jabuke	apples
jagode	strawberries
jaja sa slaninom	bacon and eggs
jaja sa šunkom	ham and eggs
jaja u aspiku	eggs in aspic
jaja u majonezu	egg mayonnaise
jaje na oko	fried eggs
janjeća jetra na žaru	grilled lamb's liver
janjeće pečenje	roast lamb
janjeći kotlet	lamb chop
janjetina	lamb
jarebica	partridge
jastog	lobster
jegulja	eel
jesetra	sturgeon
jetra	liver
jetrena pašteta	liver pâté
juha	soup
juha od gljiva	mushroom soup
juha od kupusa	cabbage soup
juha od povrća	vegetable soup
juha od rajčica	tomato soup
juneći odrezak u povrću s prilogom	beef with vegetables and garnish
junetina	beef
kačkavalj	hard full-fat cheese

kajgana	scrambled eggs
kajmak	a rich creamy cheese
kajsije	apricots
kajsijevača	apricot brandy
kakao	cocoa
kamenice	oysters
kamenice sa limunom	oysters with lemon
karfiol	cauliflower
kasato	cassata
kaštradina	smoked mutton cooked with cabbage, potatoes and beans
kava	coffee
kelj	savoy cabbage
kesten	chestnut
kesten pire	chestnut purée
kikiriki	peanuts
kisela voda	mineral water
kisele paprike	pickled peppers
kiselo mlijeko	sour milk
kiselo vrhnje	sour cream
klekovača	plum brandy with juniper
knedla	dumpling
knedle sa kajsijama	apricot dumplings
knedle sa marelicama	apricot dumplings
knedle sa sirom	dumplings with cheese
knedle sa šljivama	plum dumplings
kobasica	sausage
komovica	grape brandy
kompot	stewed fruit; compote
kompot od ...	stewed ...
kompot od bresaka	stewed peaches
konjak	cognac
konsome	consommé
kotlet	chop
kranjska kobasica	Kranj sausage
krastavac	cucumber
krem juha od povréa	cream of vegetable soup
krempita	custard cake (squares of custard cream between two layers of flaky pastry)

krepka juha s jajem	consommé with egg
krilo	wing
krofne	doughnuts
krompir	potato(es)
krompir juha	potato soup
krompir pire	mashed potatoes
kruh	bread
kruške	pears
kruškovača	pear brandy
krvav	rare
krvavica	black pudding
kuhana govedina obložena povrćem	boiled beef with vegetables
kuhano	boiled
kukuruzno brašno	corn meal
kupine	blackberries
kupus	cabbage
leća	lentils
lepinja	type of pitta bread
leskovačka mućkalica	pork escalope with onions and hot peppers
lignja	squid
lignje na žaru	grilled squid
liker	liqueur
limun	lemon
limunada	lemonade
list	sole
lješnjaci	hazelnuts
losos	salmon
lovački đuveč	hunter's stew
lozovača	grape brandy
lubenica	watermelon
luk	onion
mahune	French beans
majoneza	mayonnaise
makovnjača	poppy seed cake
maline	raspberries
maraskino	maraschino
marelice	apricots
marmelada	jam

maslac	butter
masline	olives
maslinovo ulje	olive oil
mast	fat; lard
med	honey
medenjaci	honey biscuits
meko kuhano jaje	soft-boiled egg
miješana salata	mixed salad
miješano meso na žaru	selection of grilled meats
miješano povrće	mixed vegetables
mineralna voda	mineral water
mladi sir	fresh white cheese
miljeko	milk
mlinci	flat savoury pastry made from flour, eggs and water
mljeveno meso	minced meat
morski rakovi	sea crabs
mrkva	carrot
musaka od krompira	potato moussaka
musaka od plavih patlidžana	aubergine moussaka
mušula	mussel
naranča	orange
naravni odrezak	plain veal escalope
naravni omlet	plain omelette
na ražnju	on the spit
na roštilju	barbecued; grilled
natur šnicla	plain veal escalope
na žaru	grilled
ocat	vinegar
omlet sa šunkom	ham omelette
orahnjača	walnut cake
oranžada	orange juice
orasi	walnuts
oslić	hake
osvježavajuća pića	soft drinks
ovčiji sir	ewe cheese
ovseni kruh/hljeb	oat bread
palačinke	pancakes
palačinke sa čokoladom	pancakes with chocolate
palačinke sa džemom	pancakes with jam

palačinke sa limunom	pancakes with lemon
palačinke sa orasima	pancakes with ground walnuts
palačinke sa sirom	pancakes with cheese
palenta	polenta
paprika	red or green pepper
paradajz	tomato
pariski odrezak	veal or pork escalope in batter
pastrmka	trout
pastrmka na žaru	grilled trout
pasulj	beans
paški sir	dry, hard cheese (from the island of Pag)
paticada	Dalmatian stewed beef with chard and potato
patka	duck
patlidžan	aubergine
pecivo	roll; bun
pečen	roast
pečena patka	roast duck
pečena piletina	roast chicken
pečena purica s mlincima	roast turkey with "mlinci"
pečena raca s mlincima	roast duck with "mlinci"
pečene paprike	fried peppers
pečeni krompir	roast potatoes
pečeni puran sa mlincima	roast turkey with "mlinci"
pečeno jaje	fried egg
pečurke	mushrooms
pečurke na žaru	grilled mushrooms
pekmez	jam
peršun	parsley
pileća juha	chicken soup
pileći paprikaš	chicken stew
pileći paprikaš sa noklicama	chicken stew with small dumplings
pileći paprikaš sa rezancima	chicken stew with noodles
pileći pilav	chicken pilaf
pile na roštilju	barbecued chicken
piletina	chicken
pire od spanaća	creamed spinach
pirjan	braised
pirjana teletina	braised veal

pita sa jabukama	apple pie
pita sa trešnjama	cherry pie
pita sa višnjama	morello cherry pie
pivo	beer
pjenušavo vino	sparkling wine
pljeskavica s lukom	spicy beefburger with onions
pogača	type of flat round bread
pogačice sa čvarcima	flat buns with crackling
pohan	in batter or breadcrumbs and fried
pohana piletina	fried chicken in batter
pohana teletina	breaded veal
pohane lignje	squid in batter
pohani mozak	brains in batter
pohani sir	breaded fried cheese
polubijeli kruh/hljeb	semi-white bread
pomfrit	chips
poriluk	leeks
poriluk varivo	stewed leeks
povrće	vegetables
prebranac	baked beans with onions
predjela	hors d'oeuvre
prepelica	quail
proja	corn bread
prokulice	Brussels sprouts
proso	millet
prstac	date shell, like a miniature mussel
pršut	smoked ham
pržen	fried
pržena riba	fried fish
pržene domaće kobasice	fried home-made sausages
pržene lignje	fried squid
prženi krompirići	fried potatoes
prženo jaje	fried egg
pšenični kruh/hljeb	wheat bread
pšenično brašno	wheat flour
punjen	stuffed
punjene lignje	stuffed squid
punjene paprike	stuffed peppers
punjene tikvice	stuffed marrows
punjeno u ...	bottled in ...

puran	turkey
ragout juha od teletine	veal ragout soup
rajčica	tomato
rakija	brandy
ražev kruh/hljeb	rye bread
ražnjići	kebab
rebra	ribs
restan	sautéd with onions
restan krompir	potatoes sautéd with onions
rezanci	tagliatelle
rezanci za juha	noodle soup
riba na gradele	barbecued fish
ribizle	blackcurrants
riblja čorba	fish soup
ričet	thick barley broth
ringlice	anchovy fillets
rizi-bizi	rice with peas
riža	rice
roštilj	barbecue
rotkvica	radish
ruska salata	Russian salad
ružica	rosé wine
salata od kiselih krastavaca	pickled gherkin salad
salata od kiselog kupusa	soured cabbage salad
salata od krastavaca	cucumber salad
salata od krompira	potato salad
salata od paradajza	tomato salad
salata od rajčice	tomato salad
salata od svježeg kupusa	cabbage salad
sarma	stuffed cabbage leaves
sataraš	stew made of onions, tomatoes, peppers and eggs
savijača	strudel
savijača sa jabukama	apple strudel
savijača sa sirom	cottage cheese strudel
senf	mustard
servirati hladno	serve cold
sipa	cuttlefish
sir	cheese
sir s vrhnjem	cottage cheese with sour cream

skuša	mackerel
slačica	mustard
sladoled	ice cream
sladoled od banane	banana ice cream
sladoled od jagoda	strawberry ice cream
sladoled od limuna	lemon ice cream
sladoled od lješnika	hazelnut ice cream
sladoled od malina	raspberry ice cream
sladoled od vanilije	vanilla ice cream
sladoled s tučenim vrhnjem	ice cream with whipped cream
slanina	bacon
slani štapići	savoury sticks
slatko vino	sweet wine
smokve	figs
smuđ	perch
soja	soya beans
sok od ananasa	pineapple juice
sok od borovnice	blackcurrant juice
sok od breskve	peach juice
sok od jabuke	apple juice
sok od jagode	strawberry juice
sok od kajsije	apricot juice
sok od maline	raspberry juice
sok od marelice	apricot juice
sok od naranče	orange juice
sok od paradajza	tomato juice
sok od rajčice	tomato juice
sok od višnje	sour cherry juice
sol	salt
som	catfish
somun	type of pitta bread
srnetina	venison
srpska salata	Serbian salad (tomatoes, cucumbers, onions, peppers)
stono vino	table wine
suho vino	dry wine
svinjetina	pork
svinjska krmenadla	pork chop
svinjska vješalica	grilled pork fillet
svinjski ražnjići	pork kebab

svinjski kotlet	pork chop
svinjski kotleti na samoborski	pork chops in garlic sauce
svinjsko pečenje	roast pork
šampita	squares of soft meringue between two layers of pastry
šaran	carp
šaran na roštilju	grilled carp
šatobrijan za dvije osobe	châteaubriand steak for two persons
šećer	sugar
škampi na buzaru	scampi buzara style (in tomato sauce)
šljive	plums
šljivovica	plum brandy
šnenokle	floating island (dessert)
šopska salata	Šopska salad (mixed salad with cheese)
špageti	spaghetti
šparoga	asparagus
špinat	spinach
štanglice od badema	almond pastry
štrudla od jabuka	apple strudel
štrudla od višanja	morello cherry strudel
štruklji	sweet or savoury pastry, boiled with curd cheese filling served with sour cream
štuka	pike
šumske jagode	wild strawberries
šunka	ham
šunka sa hrenom	ham with horseradish
šunka s jajima	ham and eggs
tarator	cucumber with soured milk
tartar-sos	sauce tartar
tartufi	truffles
teleća vješalica	grilled veal fillet
teleće pečenje	roast veal
teleći kotlet	veal chop
teleći medaljon	fillet of veal
teleći odrezak	veal escalope
teleći paprikaš	veal stew
teleći ragu	veal ragout

teletina	veal
tikvica	marrow
torta	gâteau
trapist	trappist cheese (similar to Port Salut)
travarica	brandy made from herbs
travnički sir	Travnik cheese (white sheep's cheese)
trešnje	cherries
tučeno vrhnje	whipped cream
tunj	tuna
turska kava	Turkish coffee
ulje	oil
umak	sauce
urmašice	finger-shaped cakes in syrup
u umaku	with sauce
vinjak	wine brandy
vino	wine
viski	whisky
višnje	morello cherries
voće	fruit
voćna salata	fruit salad
voćni kolač	fruit cake
voćni pehar	fruit coupe
voćni sok	fruit juice
voda za piće	drinking water
vrhnje	cream
zakuska	mixed starter (smoked ham, salami, cheese etc)
zelena salata	lettuce
zeljanica	spinach pie
žemička	roll; bun
žestoka pića	spirits

SHOPPING

The usual opening hours for shops are 7.30 a.m. until 12.00 noon
and 5.00 p.m. until 7.30 p.m. during the week and from 7.30 a.m.
until 2.00 p.m. on Saturdays. You will find that these opening hours
are closely adhered to in smaller places, although in bigger towns
and resorts many shops stay open right through the day. This applies
in particular to food shops which may stay open on Sundays as well.
There is nearly always a fairly large self-service mini-market or
'samoposluga' *[samoposlooga]* where you can buy groceries and house-
hold goods. Most places will also have an open-air food market,
a 'tržnica' *[tuhrɉnitsa]* or 'plac' *[plats]* where small farmers sell their
fruit, vegetables, cheese, eggs etc.

Yugoslavia has a long tradition of handicrafts and there are still
many beautiful things being made which bear the characteristics
of the rich Yugoslav folklore. In larger towns and tourist resorts there
are folk craft shops or 'narodna radinost' *[narodna radinost]* where
you can buy embroidered linen, lace, knitted garments and many
other souvenirs. Other articles to look out for are filigree silver, cut
glass and brightly coloured, geometrically patterned, flat-woven
woollen kilim rugs. Handicraft goods can also be bought in the open
markets – and this is the one time that you should try to bargain
a little with the vendors.

Foreign newspapers can be bought at newsstands in the larger
resorts and towns – as well as in hotel lobbies. Foreign books can
usually only be found in bookshops in the larger towns.

USEFUL WORDS AND PHRASES

baker	pekar	*pekar*
boutique	butik	*bootik*
butcher	mesnica	*mesnitsa*
bookshop	knjižara	*kuh-nyiɉara*
to buy	kupiti	*koopiti*
cake shop	slastičarna	*slasticharna*

cheap	jeftino	*yeftino*
chemist	apoteka	*apoteka*
department store	robna kuća	*robna koocha*
embroidery	vez	*vez*
fashion	moda	*moda*
filigree silver	filigran	*filigran*
fishmonger	ribarnica	*ribarnitsa*
florist	cvječarna	*tsuh-vye-charna*
grocer	živezne namirnice	*jivezneh namirnitseh*
ironmonger	željeznarija	*jelyeznariya*
kilim rug	čilim	*chilim*
lace	čipka	*chipka*
ladies' wear	ženska konfekcija	*jenska konfektsi-ya*
market	plac, tržnica	*plats, tuhrjnitsa*
menswear	muška konfekcija	*mooshka konfektsi-ya*
newsagent	kiosk	*kiosk*
receipt	račun	*rachoon*
record shop	prodavaonica ploča	*prodava-onitsa plocha*
sale	rasprodaja	*rasprodia*
shoe shop	prodavaonica cipela	*prodava-onitsa tsipela*
shop	prodavaonica	*prodava-onitsa*
to go shopping	ići u kupovinu	*ichi oo koopovinoo*
souvenir shop	prodavaonica suvenira	*prodava-onitsa soovenira*
special offer	reklamna cijena	*reklamna tsi-yena*
to spend	trošiti	*troshiti*
stationer	papirnica	*papirnitsa*
supermarket	samoposluga	*samoposlooga*
tailor	krojač	*kroyach*
till	kasa	*kasa*
toyshop	prodavaonica igračaka	*prodava-onitsa igrachaka*
travel agent	putnička agencija	*pootnichka agentsi-ya*
Turkish coffee pot	džezva	*jezva*

I'd like …
Želio *(men)*/željela *(women)* bih …
jeli-o/jelyela biH

Do you have …?
Imate li …?
imateh li

How much is this?
Koliko ovo košta?
koliko ovo koshta

I'll give you … dinars
Dat ću vam … dinara
dat choo vam … dinara

Oh no, that's too much
Ne, to je previše
Ne to ye previsheh

Two for …
Dva za …
duh-va za …

OK, I'll take it
Dobro, uzet ću
dobro oozet choo

Where is the … department?
Gdje je odjel za …?
guhd-ye ye odyel za

Do you have any more of these?
Imate li još?
imateh li yosh

SHOPPING

Have you anything cheaper?
Imate li nešto jeftinije?
imateh li neshto yeftini-ye

Have you anything larger/smaller?
Imate li veći/manji broj?
imateh li vechi/man-yi broy

Does it come in other colours?
Imate li ovo u drugim bojama?
imateh li ovo oo droogim boyama

Can I try it (them) on?
Smijem li ga/je (ih) probati?
smiyem li ga/ye (iH) probati

Could you wrap it for me?
Hoćete li mi ga zamotati molim?
Hocheteh li mi ga zamotati molim

Can I have a receipt?
Dajte mi račun molim vas
dīteh mi rachoon molim vas

Can I have a bag please?
Molio *(men)*/molila *(women)* bih vrećicu?
moli-o/molila biH vuh-rechitsoo

Where do I pay?
Gdje platim?
guhd-ye platim

I'd like to change this please
Htio *(men)*/htjela *(women)* bih ovo zamijeniti molim
Huh-tio/Huh-tyela biH ovo zamiyeniti molim

Can I have a refund?
Možete li mi vratiti novac?
mojeteh li mi vuh-ratiti novats

I'm just looking
Samo gledam
samo gledam

I'll come back later
Vratit ću se kasnije
vuh-ratit choo se kasniyeh

REPLIES YOU MAY BE GIVEN

Dobivate?
Are you being served?

Imate li sitno?
Have you any smaller money?

Žao mi je, rasprodano je
I'm sorry, we're out of stock

Ovo je sve što imamo
This is all we have

Dobro, dat ću vam za ...
All right, I'll let you have it for ...

Ne, ne može
No, that's impossible

Želite li nešto drugo?
Will there be anything else?

THINGS YOU'LL SEE

cijena	price
cvijeće	flowers
duhan	tobacconist
igračke	toys
kat	floor
knjižara	bookshop
krznarija	fur shop
ljetna rasprodaja	summer sale
mesnica	butcher
moda	fashion
molim ne dirati	please do not touch
muška konfekcija	menswear
muška odjeća	men's clothing
narodna radinost	folk craft shop
odjel	department
papirnica	stationer
pekara	bakery
po povoljnjoj cijeni	bargain
povrće	vegetables
prodavaonica cipela	shoe shop
putnička agencija	travel agent
reklamna cijena	special offer
robna kuća	department store
samoposluga	self-service
sladoled	ice creams
slastičarna	cake shop
sniženo	reduced
sredstva za čišćenje	household cleaning materials
tržnica	market
ženska konfekcija	ladies' clothing
ženski odjel	ladies' department
živezne namirnice	groceries

AT THE HAIRDRESSER

Hairdressers in Yugoslavia are much the same as elsewehere in Europe. A ladies' hairdresser or 'frizerski salon' will sometimes also offer various beauty treatments. Men go to a barber's shop or 'brijačnica' *[briyachnitsa]*. Unisex hairdressers are rarely found.

USEFUL WORDS AND PHRASES

appointment	dogovor	*dogovor*
beard	brada	*brada*
blond	plava	*plava*
blow dry	fen frizura	*fen frizoora*
brush	četka	*chetka*
comb	češalj	*cheshal-yuh*
conditioner	regenerator	*regenerator*
curlers	vikleri, navijači za kosu	*vikleri, naviyachi za kosoo*
curling tongs	električni uvijač	*elektrichni ooviyach*
curly	kovrčavo	*kovuhr-chavo*
dark	tamno	*tamno*
dry	osušiti	*osooshiti*
fringe	šiške	*shishkeh*
gel	gel za kosu	*gel za kosoo*
hair	kosa	*kosa*
haircut	šišanje	*shishan-ye*
hairdresser	frizer	*frizer*
hairdryer	fen	*fen*
highlights	pramenovi	*pramenovi*
long	dugo	*doogo*
moustache	brkovi	*buhr-kovi*
parting	razdjeljak	*raz-dye-lyak*
perm	trajna	*trīna*
shampoo	šampon	*shampon*
shave	obrijati	*ob-riyati*

AT THE HAIRDRESSER

shaving foam	pjena za brijanje	*pyena za bri-yan-ye*
short	kratko	*kratko*
styling mousse	pjena za kosu	*pyena za kosoo*
wash	pranje	*pran-ye*
wash and set	pranje i frizura	*pran-ye i frizoora*
wavy	valovito	*valovito*

I'd like to make an appointment
Htjela bih se dogovoriti
Huh-tyela biH se dogovoriti

Just a trim please
Samo mi podšišajte kosu molim vas
samo mi pod-shishīteh kosoo molim vas

Not too much off
Nemojte previše skratiti
nemoyteh previsheh suh-kratiti

A bit more off here please
Malo mi više skratite ovdje molim vas
malo mi visheh suh-kratiteh ovd-ye molim vas

I'd like a cut and blow-dry
Želim šišanje i fen frizuru
jelim shishan-ye i fen frizooroo

I'd like a perm
Želim trajnu
jelim trīnoo

I'd like highlights
Želim pramenove
jelim pramenoveh

THINGS YOU'LL SEE OR HEAR

brijačnica	barber's
fen frizura	blow-dry
frizer	hair stylist, hairdresser
frizerski salon	hairdressing salon
frizer za muškarce	men's hairdresser
frizura	set
kolor šampon	tint
trajna	perm
ženski frizerski salon	ladies' salon

Kako želite?
How would you like it?

Da li je to dovoljno kratko?
Is that short enough?

Hoćete li regenerator?
Would you like any conditioner?

Da li ste zadovoljni?
Are you pleased with it?

SPORT

Yugoslavia has 1,000 kilometres of coastline, providing excellent opportunities for swimming, water-skiing, sailing, sailboarding and fishing. With its 365 different kinds of fish, the Adriatic is a fisherman's paradise, although the daily catch is limited to 5kg. Both sea-fishing from a boat and underwater fishing are governed by certain restrictions as to the type of equipment used, the fishing site etc., and you must either obtain a permit from the local municipal authority or join one of the appropriate Yugoslav fishing or diving associations. Sea-angling on the Adriatic coast does not require a permit, but freshwater fishing does – again, the local council, angling club or even your hotel may provide this. The many rivers and lakes abound in trout, 'pastrva' *[pastuhrva]*, and salmon, 'losos' *[losos]*, etc., and the country's mountains, forests and plains have plenty of game. Hunting is well-organized for tourists, with guides and wardens available.

All foreign boats must be registered at the nearest harbour, and a sailing permit obtained, as soon as possible after entering Yugoslav territorial waters. Scuba diving needs special permission.

Ski resorts are plentiful in Slovenia and are becoming well-developed in other areas; ice-skating is popular, and the many fast-flowing rivers provide excellent canoeing. Facilities for games such as basketball and handball can be found in most major towns, tennis is beginning to catch on, and golf courses are on the increase. As in most European countries, football is probably the most popular spectator sport.

USEFUL WORDS AND PHRASES

athletics	atletika	*atletika*
badminton	badminton	*badminton*
ball	lopta	*lopta*
beach	plaža	*plaʒa*
bicycle	bicikl	*bitsikuhl*
canoe	kanu	*kanoo*

canoeing	kanuing	*kanooing*
deckchair	ležaljka	*leźaȳuh-ka*
diving board	odskočna daska	*odskochna daska*
fishing	ribolov	*ribolov*
fishing rod	štap za pecanje	*shtap za petsa-nye*
flippers	peraje	*peri-e*
football	nogomet/fudbal	*nogomet/foodbal*
football match	nogometna utakmica	*nogometna ootakmitsa*
goggles	maska za ronjenje	*maska za ron-yen-ye*
golf	golf	*golf*
golf course	teren za golf	*teren za golf*
gymnastics	gimnastika	*gimnastika*
harpoon	harpun	*Harpoon*
hockey	hokej	*Hokay*
jogging	jogging	*joging*
lake	jezero	*yezero*
mountaineering	planinarenje	*planinaren-ye*
oxygen bottles	boca sa kisikom	*botsa sa kisikom*
pedal boat	čamac na pedale	*chamats na pedaleh*
racket	reket	*reket*
riding	jahanje	*yahan-ye*
rowing boat	čamac	*chamats*
to run	trčati	*tuhr-chati*
sailboard	daska za jedrenje	*daska za yedren-ye*
sailing	jedrenje	*yedren-ye*
sand	pijesak	*pi-yesak*
sea	more	*moreh*
to skate	klizati	*klizati*
skates	klizaljke	*klizal-yuh-ke*
skin diving	podvodno ronjenje	*podvodno ron-yen-ye*
snorkel	disaljka	*disal-yuh-ka*
stadium	stadion	*stadi-on*
sunshade	suncobran	*soontsobran*
to swim	plivati	*plivati*
swimming pool	bazen	*bazen*
tennis	tenis	*tenis*
tennis court	tenisko igralište	*tenisko igralishteh*

tennis racket	reket za tenis	*reket za tenis*
tent	šator	*shator*
underwater fishing	podvodni ribolov	*podvodni ribolov*
volleyball	odbojka	*odboyka*
walking	hodanje	*Hodan-ye*
water skiing	skijanje na vodi	*ski-yanyeh na vodi*
water skis	skije za vodu	*skiyeh za vodoo*
wave	val	*val*
wet suit	ronilačko odijelo	*ronilachko odi-yelo*
yacht	jahta, jedrilica	*yaHta, yedrilitsa*

How do I get to the beach?
Kako se dođe do plaže?
kako se dojeh do plajeh

How deep is the water here?
Koliko je duboka voda ovdje?
koliko ye dooboka voda ovd-ye

Is there an indoor/outdoor pool here?
Ima li zatvoren/otvoren bazen ovdje?
ima li zatvoren/otvoren bazen ovd-ye

Is it dangerous to swim here?
Da li je opasno tu plivati?
da li ye opasno too plivati

Can I fish here?
Smijem li ovdje loviti ribu?
smiyem li ovd-ye loviti riboo

Do I need a licence?
Treba li mi dozvola?
treba li mi dozvola

I'd like a fishing licence
Molim vas dozvolu za ribolov
molim vas dozvoloo za ribolov

Can you give me a sailing permit?
Možete li mi izdati dozvolu za plovidbu?
mojeteh li mi izdati dozvoloo za plovidboo

I would like to hire a sunshade
Želio *(men)*/željela *(women)* bih iznajmiti suncobran
jeli-o/jelyela biH iznīmiti soontsobran

How much does it cost per hour/day?
Koliko košta na dan/sat?
koliko koshta na dan/sat

I would like to take water-skiing lessons
Želio *(men)*/željela *(women)* bih uzimati satove iz skijanja na vodi
jeli-o/jelyela biH oozimati satoveh iz ski-yanya na vodi

Where can I hire ...?
Gdje mogu iznajmiti ...?
guhd-ye mogoo iznīmiti

THINGS YOU'LL SEE

bicikli	bicycles
hipodrom	race course
jedrilice	sailing boats
kampiranje zabranjeno	no camping
karte	tickets
lučka policija	harbour police
luka	port
nogometno igralište	football pitch
plaža	beach
plivanje zabranjeno	no swimming
prva pomoć	first aid
satovi iz skijanja na vodi	water-skiing
sportovi na vodi	water sports
sportska dvorana	sports centre
stadion	stadium
staza za bicikliste	cycle path
tenisko igralište	tennis court
zabranjeno ronjenje	no diving
zabranjen prilaz	restricted area
zabranjen ribolov	no fishing
za najam	for hire

POST OFFICES & BANKS

Post offices are easily recognized by their yellow PTT signs. Letter-boxes are also painted yellow and marked PTT. Post offices are usually open all day from 8.00 a.m. until 7.00 p.m., including Saturday. In the larger main towns they open on Sundays from 8.00 a.m. until 2.00 p.m. Poste-restante facilities are available at main post offices. Stamps can also be bought at tobacconists or 'duhan' [doohan] and kiosks. Since there are not very many public phone boxes in Yugoslavia post offices are the best place for making phonecalls.

Banks are open from 8.00 a.m. until 7.00 p.m. on weekdays and from 8.00 a.m. until noon on Saturdays. Some close for lunch from 12.30 – 1.30. You will need to show your passport when exchanging money. The basic unit of Yugoslav currency is the dinar. People have a tendency to talk in terms of 'old dinars' or 'stari dinari' [stari dinari] and 'new dinars' or 'novi dinari' [novi dinari] so you'll need to check what they mean. 1,000,000 old dinars is equivalent to 10,000 new dinars, so to convert old into new dinars you subtract 2 zeros. The actual notes and coins are, of course, new dinars.

USEFUL WORDS AND PHRASES

account	račun	rachoon
airmail	avionom	avi-onom
bank	banka	banka
banknote	novčanica	nov-chanitsa
to change	mijenjati	mi-yen-yati
cheque	ček	chek
counter	pult	poolt
customs form	carinski formular	tsarinski formoolar
delivery	dostava	dostava
deposit	kaucija	ka-ootsi-ya
exchange rate	kurs	koors
foreign currency	devize	devizeh

form	formular	*formoolar*
international	međunarodna	*mejoonarodna*
money order	uplatnica	*ooplatnitsa*
letter	pismo	*pismo*
letter box	poštanski sanduk	*poshtanski sandook*
mail	pošta	*poshta*
money order	uplatnica	*ooplatnitsa*
package, parcel	paket	*paket*
post	pošta	*poshta*
postage rates	poštarina	*poshtarina*
postal order	uplatnica	*ooplatnitsa*
postcard	razglednica	*raz-glednitsa*
postcode	poštanski broj	*poshtanski broy*
poste-restante	poste-restante	*post-restant*
postman	poštar	*poshtar*
post office	pošta	*poshta*
pound sterling	funta	*foonta*
registered letter	preporučeno pismo	*preporoocheno pismo*
stamp	marka	*marka*
surface mail	obična pošta	*obichna poshta*
telegram	telegram	*telegram*
traveller's cheque	putnički ček	*pootnichki chek*

How much is a letter/postcard to …?
Koliko dođe marka za pismo/razglednicu za …?
koliko dojeh marka za pismo/raz-glednitsoo za

I would like three … dinar stamps
Tri marke po … dinara molim
tri markeh po … dinara molim

I want to register this letter
Želim ovo pismo poslati preporučenom poštom
jelim ovo pismo poslati preporoochenom poshtom

I want to send this parcel to ...
Želim ovaj paket poslati u ...
jelim ovī paket poslati oo

How long does the post to ... take?
Koliko dugo treba da stigne do ...?
koliko doogo treba da stigneh do

Where can I post this?
Gdje ovo mogu poslati poštom?
guh-dye ovo mogoo poslati poshtom

Is there any mail for me?
Ima li za mene pošte?
ima li za meneh poshteh

I'd like to send a telegram
Želim poslati telegram
jelim poslati telegram

This is to go airmail
Ovo treba ići avionom
ovo treba ichi avi-onom

I'd like to change this into ...
Želim promijeniti ovo u ...
jelim promiyeniti ovo oo

Can I cash these traveller's cheques?
Mogu li unovčiti ove putničke čekove?
mogoo li oonovchiti oveh pootnichkeh chekoveh

What is the exchange rate for the pound?
Koji je tečaj za englesku funtu?
koyi ye techī za engleskoo foontoo

THINGS YOU'LL SEE

adresa	address
avionom	airmail
blagajnik	cashier
cijena	charge
dopisnica	postcard
hitno, ekspres	express
inozemna poštarina	postage abroad
ispuniti	to fill in
kupovni tečaj	we buy
kurs	exchange rate
marka	stamp
mjenjačnica	foreign exchange
mjesto	place
paket	packet
pismo	letter
pošiljalac	sender
pošta	post office
poštanski broj	post code
poštanski sanduk	letterbox
poštarina	postage
preporučeno pismo	registered mail
prima	addressee
prodaja maraka	stamps
prodajni tečaj	we sell
PTT	post office; letterbox
radno vrijeme	opening hours
razglednica	picture postcard
šalter za pakete	parcels counter
tečaj	exchange rate
telegrami	telegrams
tuzemna poštarina	inland postage
uplatnice	money orders

TELEPHONES

Yugoslavia has an automated telephone system and it is possible to make direct calls to virtually anywhere in the world. However, there are not many public call boxes. If you want to make an international call it is best to go to a post office (PTT) where the operator will make the connection for you and direct you to a numbered cabin for the conversation. When you have finished you pay the operator according to the time taken.

To call the UK direct, dial 99 44 followed by the UK area code (omitting the 0 which prefixes this), then the number you want. To call the USA dial 99 1 followed by area code and telephone number, again omitting any initial 0. The Yugoslav dialling tone is made up of a short tone followed by a longer tone; a repeated long tone means that the number is ringing out; repeated short tones indicate an engaged number.

USEFUL WORDS AND PHRASES

call	poziv	*poziv*
to call	pozvati	*pozvati*
code	pozivni broj	*pozivni broy*
crossed line	netko je upao u razgovor	*netko ye oopa-o oo razgovor*
to dial	birati broj	*birati broy*
dialling tone	pozivni ton	*pozivni ton*
emergency	u slučaju opasnosti	*oo sloochīu opasnosti*
enquiries	informacije	*informatsiyeh*
extension	kučni broj	*koochnī broy*
international call	međunarodni poziv	*mejoonarodni poziv*
number	broj	*broy*
operator	operater	*operater*
pay-phone	telefon na ubacivanje novčića	*telefon na oobatsivan-ye novchicha*
receiver	slušalica	*slooshalitsa*

reverse **charge call**	poziv na njihov račun	*poziv na nyiHov rachoon*
telephone	telefon	*telefon*
telephone box	telefonska govornica	*telefonska govornitsa*
telephone directory	telefonski imenik	*telefonski imenik*
wrong number	pogrešan broj	*pogreshan broy*

Where is the nearest phone box?
Gdje se nalazi najbliža telefonska govornica?
guh-dye se nalazi nīblīja telefonska govornitsa

Is there a telephone directory?
Ima li telefonski imenik?
ima li telefonski imenik

I would like the directory for ...
Molim vas imenik za ...?
molim vas imenik za

Can I call abroad from here?
Mogu li nazvati inozemstvo odavde?
mogoo li nazvati inozemstvo odavdeh

I want to call this number in Britain
Želim nazvati ovaj broj u Engleskoj
jelim nazvati ovī broy oo engleskoy

How much is a call to ...?
Koliko košta telefonski razgovor sa ...?
koliko koshta telefonski razgovor sa

I would like to reverse the charges
Želim nazvati na njihov račun
jelim nazvati na nyiHov rachoon

I would like a number in ...
Želim nazvati broj u ...
jelim nazvati broy oo ...

Hello, this is ... speaking
Halo, ovdje ...
Halo ovd-ye

Is that ...?
Da li je to ...?
da li ye to

Speaking
Na telefonu
na telefonoo

I would like to speak to ...
Želim razgovarati s ...
jelim razgovarati suh

Extension ... please
Kućni ..., molim
koochni ... molim

Please tell him ... called
Molim vas recite mu da je ... zvao
molim vas retsiteh moo da ye ... zva-o

Ask him to call me back please
Molim vas, recite mu da me nazove
molim vas retsiteh moo da me nazoveh

My number is ...
Moj je broj ...
moy ye broy

TELEPHONES

Do you know where he is?
Da li znate gdje se on nalazi?
da li znateh guh-dye se on nalazi

When will he be back?
Kada se vraća?
kada se vracha

Could you leave him a message?
Možete li mu ostaviti poruku?
mojeteh li moo ostaviti porookoo

I'll ring back later
Kasnije ću zvati
kasniyeh choo zvati

Sorry, wrong number
Žao mi je, dobio sam pogrešan broj
jao mi ye dobio sam pogreshan broy

THINGS YOU'LL SEE

cijene	charges
gradski poziv	local call
informacije	enquiries
izravno biranje broja	direct dialling
međunarodni	international
međunarodni poziv	international call
međugradski poziv	long-distance call
ne radi	out of order
pošta	post office
pozivni broj	code
PTT	post office
telefonska govornica	telephone box
u slučaju opasnosti	emergency

REPLIES YOU MAY BE GIVEN

Molim vas otiđite u kabinu 7
Please go to cabin number 7

S kim želite razgovarati?
Who would you like to speak to?

Dobili ste pogrešan broj
You've got the wrong number

Tko govori?
Who's speaking?

Koji je vaš broj?
What is your number?

Žao mi je, nema ga
Sorry, he's not in

Vraća se u ... sati
He'll be back at ... o'clock

Molim vas nazovite sutra
Please call again tomorrow

Reći ću mu da ste zvali
I'll tell him you called

HEALTH

Yugoslavia has a convention with the UK covering health care and this entitles British citizens to free medical treatment. Non-Europeans must pay (or be insured) but the charges are very reasonable. Most doctors speak English. Chemists are open during normal shopping hours (see SHOPPING) but also operate a rota system so that there is always a duty chemist open. The rota is published in the local newspaper.

USEFUL WORDS AND PHRASES

accident	nesreća	*nes-recha*
ambulance	kola hitne pomoći	*kola Hitneh pomochi*
anaemic	anemičan	*anemichan*
appendicitis	upala slijepog crijeva	*oopala sli-yepog tsri-yeva*
appendix	slijepo crijevo	*sli-yepo tsri-yevo*
aspirin	aspirin	*aspirin*
asthma	astma	*astma*
backache	bol u leđima	*bol oo lejima*
bandage	zavoj	*zavoy*
bite *(by dog)*	ujed	*ooyed*
(by insect)	ubod	*oobod*
bladder	mjehur	*myeHoor*
blister	plik	*plik*
blood	krv	*kuhrv*
blood donor	davalac krvi	*davalats kuhrvi*
burn	opekotina	*opekotina*
cancer	rak	*rak*
check-up	pregled	*preg-led*
chemist	ljekarna, apoteka	*lyekarna, apoteka*
chest	grudi	*groodi*
chickenpox	vodene kozice	*vodeneh kozitseh*
cold	prehlada	*preHlada*
concussion	potres mozga	*potres mozga*

constipation	konstipacija	*konstipatsiya*
contact lenses	kontaktne leće	*kontaktneh lecheh*
corn	kurjeoko	*kooryeh-oko*
cough *(noun)*	kašalj	*kashal-yuh*
cut	rez	*rez*
dentist	zubar	*zoobar*
diabetes	diabetes, šećerna bolest	*diabetes, shecherna bolest*
diarrhoea	proljev	*pro-lyev*
dizzy	vrtoglavica	*vuhrtoglavitsa*
doctor	liječnik, doktor	*liyechnik, doktor*
earache	uhobolja	*ooHobolya*
fever	groznica	*groznitsa*
filling	plomba	*plomba*
first aid	prva pomoć	*puhrva pomoch*
flu	gripa	*gripa*
fracture	napukla kost	*napookla kost*
German measles	rubeola	*roobeh-ola*
glasses	naočale	*na-ochaleh*
haemorrhage	hemeroidi	*Hemero-idi*
hayfever	peludna groznica	*peloodna groznitsa*
headache	glavobolja	*glavobolya*
heart	srce	*suhr-tse*
heart attack	srčani udar	*suhrchani oodar*
hospital	bolnica	*bolnitsa*
ill	bolestan	*bolestan*
indigestion	loša probava	*losha probava*
infected	inficirano	*infitsirano*
injection	injekcija	*inyek-tsiya*
itch	svrbež	*suh-vuhr-bej*
kidney	bubreg	*boobreg*
lump	kvrga	*kuh-vuhr-ga*
measles	ospice	*ospitseh*
migraine	migrena	*migrena*
mumps	mumps	*moomps*
nausea	mučnina	*moochnina*
nurse	medicinska sestra	*meditsinska sestra*

89

operation	operacija	*operatsiya*
optician	okulista	*okoolista*
pain	bol	*bol*
penicillin	penicilin	*penitsilin*
plaster *(sticky)*	flaster	*flaster*
plaster of Paris	gips	*gips*
pneumonia	upala pluća	*oopala ploocha*
pregnant	trudna	*troodna*
prescription	recept	*retsept*
rheumatism	reuma	*re-ooma*
scald	opekotina	*opekotina*
scratch	ogrebotina	*ogrebotina*
smallpox	male boginje	*maleh bogin-ye*
sore throat	upaljeno grlo	*oopalyeno guhr-lo*
splinter	iverak	*iverak*
sprain	iščašenje	*ish-cha-shen-ye*
sting	ubod	*oobod*
stomach	želudac, stomak	*jeloodats, stomak*
temperature	temperatura	*temperatoora*
tonsils	krajnici	*krinitsi*
toothache	zubobolja	*zoobobolya*
travel sickness	putna groznica	*pootna groznitsa*
ulcer	čir	*chir*
vaccination	vakcinacija	*vak-tsinatsiya*
to vomit	povraćati	*povrachati*
whooping cough	hripavac	*Hripavats*

I have a pain in …
Boli me …
boli me

I do not feel well
Loše se osjećam
losheh se osyecham

I feel faint
Slabo se osjećam
slabo se osyecham

I feel sick
Zlo mi je
zuh-lo mi ye

I feel dizzy
Vrti mi se u glavi
vuhrti mi se oo glavi

It hurts here
Ovdje me boli
ovd-ye me boli

It's a sharp pain
Oštra je bol
oshtra ye bol

It's a dull pain
Tupa je bol
toopa ye bol

It hurts all the time
Stalno boli
stalno boli

It only hurts now and then
Boli me samo povremeno
boli me samo povremeno

It hurts when you touch it
Boli me kada se dodirne
boli me kada se dodirneh

It hurts more at night
Više boli noću
visheh boli nochoo

It stings
Peće
pecheh

It aches
Boli
boli

I have a temperature
Imam temperaturu
imam temperatooroo

I need a prescription for ...
Treba mi recept za ...
treba mi retsept za

I normally take ...
Obično uzimam ...
obichno oozimam

I'm allergic to ...
Alergičan sam na ...
alergichan sam na

Have you got anything for ...?
Imate li što za ...?
imateh li shto za

Do I need a prescription for ...?
Da li mi treba recept za ...?
da li mi treba retsept za

I have lost a filling
Ispala mi je plomba
ispala mi ye plomba

REPLIES YOU MAY BE GIVEN

Popijte po ... tableta/pilula
Take ... pills/tablets at a time

S vodom
With water

Žvačite ih
Chew them

Jedamput/dva puta/tri puta dnevno
Once/twice/three times a day

Isključivo prije spavanja
Only when you go to bed

Što obično uzimate?
What do you normally take?

Mislim da biste trebali ići kod doktora/liječnika
I think you should see a doctor

Žao mi je, toga nemamo
I'm sorry, we don't have that

Za to vam treba recept
For that you need a prescription

THINGS YOU'LL SEE

ambulanta	surgery
bolnica	hospital
dežurna ljekarna	duty chemist
hitna pomoć	emergencies
klinika	clinic
kola hitne pomoći	ambulance
krvni pritisak	blood pressure
lijek	medicine
liječnik	doctor
ljekarna	chemist
naočale	glasses
okulista	optician
otorinolaringolog	ear, nose and throat specialist
prije jela	on an empty stomach
rentgen	X-ray
recept	prescription
stanica za hitnu pomoć	first aid post
tlak	blood pressure
zubar	dentist
zubno meso	gum

CONVERSION TABLES

DISTANCES

Distances are marked in kilometres. To convert kilometres to miles, divide the km. by 8 and multiply by 5 (one km. being five-eighths of a mile). Convert miles to km. by dividing the miles by 5 and multiplying by 8. A mile is 1609m. (1.609km.).

km.	miles _or_ km.	miles
1.61	1	0.62
3.22	2	1.24
4.83	3	1.86
6.44	4	2.48
8.05	5	3.11
9.66	6	3.73
11.27	7	4.35
12.88	8	4.97
14.49	9	5.59
16.10	10	6.21
32.20	20	12.43
48.28	30	18.64
64.37	40	24.85
80.47	50	31.07
160.93	100	62.14
321.90	200	124.30
804.70	500	310.70
1609.34	1000	621.37

Other units of length:

1 centimetre = 0.39 in.	1 inch = 25.4 millimetres
1 metre = 39.37 in.	1 foot = 0.30 metre (30 cm.)
10 metres = 32.81 ft.	1 yard = 0.91 metre

WEIGHTS

The unit you will come into most contact with is the kilogram (kilo),
equivalent to 2 lb 3 oz. To convert kg. to lbs., multiply by 2 and
add one-tenth of the result (thus, 6 kg x 2 = 12 + 1.2, or 13.2 lbs).
One ounce is about 28 grams, and 1 lb is 454 g. One UK
hundredweight is almost 51 kg; one USA cwt is 45 kg. One UK
ton is 1016 kg (USA ton = 907 kg).

grams	ounces	ounces	grams
50	1.76	1	28.3
100	3.53	2	56.7
250	8.81	4	113.4
500	17.63	8	226.8

kg.	lbs. or kg.	lbs.
0.45	1	2.20
0.91	2	4.41
1.36	3	6.61
1.81	4	8.82
2.27	5	11.02
2.72	6	13.23
3.17	7	15.43
3.63	8	17.64
4.08	9	19.84
4.53	10	22.04
9.07	20	44.09
11.34	25	55.11
22.68	50	110.23
45.36	100	220.46

LIQUIDS

Motorists from the UK will be used to seeing petrol priced per litre (and may even know that one litre is about $1\frac{3}{4}$ pints). One 'imperial' gallon is roughly $4\frac{1}{2}$ litres, but USA drivers must remember that the American gallon is only 3.8 litres (1 litre = 1.06 US quart). In the following table, imperial gallons are used:

litres	gals. *or* l.	gals.
4.54	1	0.22
9.10	2	0.44
13.64	3	0.66
18.18	4	0.88
22.73	5	1.10
27.27	6	1.32
31.82	7	1.54
36.37	8	1.76
40.91	9	1.98
45.46	10	2.20
90.92	20	4.40
136.38	30	6.60
181.84	40	8.80
227.30	50	11.00

TYRE PRESSURES

lb/sq.in.	15	18	20	22	24
kg/sq.cm.	1.1	1.3	1.4	1.5	1.7

lb/sq.in.	26	28	30	33	35
kg/sq.cm.	1.8	2.0	2.1	2.3	2.5

CONVERSION TABLES

AREA

The average tourist isn't all that likely to need metric area conversions, but with more 'holiday home' plots being bought overseas nowadays it might be useful to know that 1 square metre = 10.8 square feet, and that the main unit of land area measurement is a hectare (which is $2\frac{1}{2}$ acres). The hectare is 10,000 sq.m. – for convenience, visualise something roughly 100 metres or yards square. To convert hectares to acres, divide by 2 and multiply by 5 (and vice-versa).

hectares	acres or ha.	acres
0.4	**1**	2.5
2.0	**5**	12.4
4.1	**10**	24.7
20.2	**50**	123.6
40.5	**100**	247.1

TEMPERATURE

To convert centigrade or Celsius degrees into Fahrenheit, the accurate method is to multiply the °C figure by 1.8 and add 32. Similarly, to convert °F to °C, subtract 32 from the °F figure and divide by 1.8. This will give you a truly accurate conversion, but takes a little time in mental arithmetic! See the table below. If all you want is some idea of how hot it is forecast to be in the sun, simply double the °C figure and add 30; the °F result will be overstated by a degree or two when the answer is in the 60-80°F range, while 90°F should be 86°F.

°C	°F	°C	°F	
-10	14	25	77	
0	32	30	86	
5	41	36.9	98.4	body temperature
10	50	40	104	
20	68	100	212	boiling point

CLOTHING SIZES

Slight variations in sizes, let alone European equivalents of UK/USA sizes, will be found everywhere so be sure to check before you buy. The following tables are approximate:

Women's dresses and suits

UK	10	12	14	16	18	20
Europe	**36**	**38**	**40**	**42**	**44**	**46**
USA	8	10	12	14	16	18

Men's suits and coats

UK/USA	36	38	40	42	44	46
Europe	**46**	**48**	**50**	**52**	**54**	**56**

Women's shoes

UK	4	5	6	7	8
Europe	**37**	**38**	**39**	**41**	**42**
USA	$5\frac{1}{2}$	$6\frac{1}{2}$	$7\frac{1}{2}$	$8\frac{1}{2}$	$9\frac{1}{2}$

Men's shoes

UK/USA	7	8	9	10	11
Europe	**41**	**42**	**43**	**44**	**45**

Men's shirts

UK/USA	14	$14\frac{1}{2}$	15	$15\frac{1}{2}$	16	$16\frac{1}{2}$	17
Europe	**36**	**37**	**38**	**39**	**41**	**42**	**43**

Women's sweaters

UK/USA	32	34	36	38	40
Europe	**36**	**38**	**40**	**42**	**44**

Waist and chest measurements

Inches	28	30	32	34	36	38	40	42	44	46
Cms	71	76	80	87	91	97	102	107	112	117

MINI-DICTIONARY

about: about 5 oko pet
accelerator ubrzavač
accident nesreća
accommodation smještaj
ache bol
adaptor *(electrical)* adaptor
address adresa
adhesive ljepilo
Adriatic Jadransko more
after poslije
after-shave lotion za poslije brijanja
again ponovno
against protiv
air-conditioning klimatizacija
aircraft avion
air freshener osvježivač zraka
air hostess stjuardesa
airline avionska kompanija
airport aerodrom
alarm clock budilica
Albania Albanska
Albanian *(man)* Albanac
 (woman) Albanka
 (adj) albanski
alcohol alkohol
all sve
 all the streets sve ulice
 that's all, thanks to bi bilo sve, hvala
almost gotovo
alone sam
already već
always uvijek
am: I am ja sam
ambulance kola hitne pomoći
America Amerika
American *(man)* Amerikanac
 (woman) Amerikanka

 (adj) američki
and i
ankle gležanj
anorak vindjakna
another *(different)* drugo
 another coffee *(additional)* još jedna kava
anti-freeze antifriz
antique shop antikvarnica
antiseptic antiseptik
apartment stan
aperitif aperitiv
appetite apetit
apple jabuka
application form prijavnica
appointment dogovor
apricot marelica
are: you are *(formal)* vi ste
 (familiar) ti si
 we are mi smo
 they are oni su
arm ruka
art umjetnost
art gallery likovna galerija
artist umjetnik
as: as soon as possible što prije
ashtray pepeljara
asleep: he's asleep on spava
aspirin aspirin
at: at the post office na pošti
 at night noću
 at 3 o'clock u tri sata
attractive zgodan
aunt tetka
Australia Australija
Australian *(man)* Australijanac
 (woman) Australijanka
 (adj) australski
Austria Austrija

Austrian *(man)* Austrijanac
  (woman) Austrijanka
  (adj) austrijski
automatic automatski
away: is it far away? da li je
  daleko?
  go away! odlazi!
awful grozno
axe sjekir
axle osovina

baby beba
back *(not front)* poleđna
  (body) leđa
bacon slanina
  bacon and eggs slanina s jajima
bad loš
bait mamac
bake peći
baker pekar
balcony balkon
ball *(football etc)* lopta
  (tennis) tenis loptica
ball-point pen penkalo
banana banana
band *(musicians)* orkestar
  (pop) pop grupa
bandage zavoj
bank banka
banknote novčanica
bar *(counter)* šank
  (in hotel) bar
  (cafe) kafić
  bar of chocolate tabla čokolade
barbecue roštilj
barber's brijačnica
bargain: it's a bargain baš je
  jeftino
basement suteren

basin *(sink)* lavabo
basket košarica
bath kada
  to have a bath okupati se
bathing hat kapa za plivanje
bathroom *(Croatian)* kupaonica;
  (Serbian) kupatilo
battery akumulator
beach plaža
beans grah
beard brada
because zato što
bed *(Croatian)* krevet;
  (Serbian) postelja
bed linen posteljina
bedroom spavaća soba
beef junetina
beer pivo
before prije
beginner početnik
behind iza
beige bež
Belgium Belgija
Belgrade Beograd
bell zvono
below ispod
belt pojas
beside pokraj
best najbolje
better bolje
between između
bicycle bicikl
big veliki
bikini bikini
bill račun
bin liner vreća za smeće
bird ptica
birthday rođendan
  happy birthday! sretan rođendan!
birthday present poklon za
  rođendan
biscuit keks

bite *(verb)* gristi
  (noun: by dog etc) ujed
  (by insect) ubod
bitter gorak
black crn
blackberry kupina
blanket pokrivač
bleach *(verb: hair)* poblajhati
  (noun: for cleaning) varikina
blind *(cannot see)* slijep
blister mjehurić
blood krv
blouse bluza
blue plav
boat brod
  (smaller) čamac
body tijelo
boil kuhati
bolt *(on door)* zasun
  to bolt the door povući zasun
  na vratima
bone kost
bonnet *(car)* hauba
book *(noun)* knjiga
  (verb) rezervirati
booking office šalter za
  rezervacije
bookshop knjižara
boot *(car)* prtljažnica
  (footwear) čizma
border granica
boring dosadno
born: I was born in ... rođen
  sam ...
both oba
  both of them obadvoje
  both of us nas oboje
  both ... and ... i ... i ...
bottle boca
bottle-opener otvarač za boce
bottom dno
  (of person) stražnica

bowl zdjela
box kutija
boy dječak
boyfriend dečko
bra prsluk
bracelet narukvica
braces naramenice
brake *(noun)* kočnica
  (verb) kočiti
brandy konjak
bread *(Croatian)* kruh
  (Serbian) hleb
breakdown *(car)* kvar
  (nervous) slom živaca
breakfast doručak
breathe disati
  I can't breathe ne mogu
  disati
bridge most
briefcase poslovna tašna
British britanski
brochure prospekt
broken slomljen
  broken leg slomljena noga
brooch broš
brother brat
brown smeđe
bruise modrica
brush *(noun)* četka
  (artist's) kist
  (verb) četkati
bucket kanta
building zgrada
Bulgaria Bugarska
Bulgarian *(man)* Bugarin
  (woman) Bugarka
  (adj) bugarski
bumper branik
burglar provalnik
burn *(verb)* goriti
  (noun) opekotina
bus autobus

bus station *(Croatian)* autobusni kolodvor
  (Serbian) autobuska stanica
business posao
  it's none of your business to se vas ne tiče
busy *(occupied)* zauzet
  (bar) gužva je
but ali
butcher mesar
butter maslac
button gumb
buy kupiti
by: by the window pokraj prozora
  by Friday do petka
  by myself sam

cabbage kupus
cable car žičara
café kavana
cake kolač
calculator računalo
call: what's it called? kako se zove?
camera fotografski aparat
campsite kampiralište
camshaft zupčanik
can *(tin)* limenka
  can I have ...? dajte mi ...
  I can't ... ne mogu ...
  can you ...? možete li ...?
Canada Kanada
Canadian *(man)* Kanađanin
  (woman) Kanađanka
  (adj) kanadski
cancer rak
candle svijeća
canoe kanu

cap *(bottle)* čep
  (hat) kapa
car kola, auto
caravan kamp-prikolica
carburettor karburator
card *(greetings)* čestitka
  (picture postcard) razglednica
  (business) posjetnica
cardigan džemper
careful pažljiv
  be careful! pazi!
carpet tepih
carriage *(train)* vagon
carrot mrkva
carry-cot prenosiva kolijevka
case *(suitcase)* kofer
cash gotovina
  (coins) kovanice
  to pay cash platiti u gotovini
cassette kazeta
cassette player kazetofon
castle zamak
cat mačka
cathedral katedrala
cauliflower karfiol
cave špilja
cemetery groblje
centre centar
chair stolica
chambermaid sobarica
chamber music komorna muzika
  (Croatian also) komorna glazba
change *(noun: money)* sitniš
  (verb: money) promijeniti
  (verb: clothes) presvući se
cheap jeftin
cheerio zdravo
cheers! živjeli!
cheese sir
chemist *(shop)* ljekarna
cheque ček
cheque book čekovna knjižica

cheque card čekovna kartica
cherry trešnja
chess šah
chest grudi
chewing gum žvakaća guma
chicken pile
child dijete
children djeca
china porculan
China Kina
Chinese *(man)* Kinez
  (woman) Kineskinja
  (adj) kineski
chips pomfrit
chocolate čokolada
  box of chocolates bomboniera
chop *(food)* krmenadla
  (to cut) nasjeckati
Christian name ime
church crkva
cigar cigara
cigarette cigareta
cinema kino
city velegrad
city centre centar grada
class klasa
classical music klasična muzika
  (Croatian also) klasična glazba
clean čist
clear *(obvious)* jasno
  (water) čisto
  is that clear? da li je to jasno?
clever pametan
clock sat
close *(near)* blizu
  (stuffy) zagušljivo
  (verb) zatvoriti
  the shop is closed prodavaonica
  je zatvorena
clothes odjeća
club klub
  (cards) tref

clutch kvačilo
coach autobus
  (of train) kupe
coach station *(Croatian)* autobusni
  kolodvor
  (Serbian) autobuska stanica
coat kaput
coathanger vješalica
cockroach žohar
coffee kava
coin novčić
cold *(illness)* prehlada
  (adj) hladan
  I'm cold hladno mi je
collar ovratnik
collection *(stamps etc)* zbirka
colour boja
colour film film u boji
comb *(noun)* češalj
  (verb) češljati
come doći
  I come from ... ja sam iz ...
  we came last week došli smo
  prošli tjedan
  come here! dođi ovamo!
compartment kupe
complicated komplicirano
concert koncert
conditioner *(hair)* regenerator
conductor *(bus)* kondukter
  (orchestra) dirigent
congratulations! čestitam!
constipation konstipacija
consulate konzulat
contact lenses kontaktne leće
contraceptive kontracepcijsko
  sredstvo
cook *(noun)* kuhar
  (verb) kuhati
cooking utensils kuhinjska oprema
cool prohladno
Corfu Krf

cork čep
corkscrew vadičep
corner ugao
corridor hodnik
cosmetics kozmetika
cost *(verb)* koštati
  what does it cost? koliko košta?
cotton pamuk
cotton wool vata
cough *(verb)* kašljati
  (noun) kašalj
country *(state)* zemlja
  (not town) selo
cousin *(male)* rođak
  (female) rođakinja
crab rak
cramp grč
crayfish slatkovodni rak
cream *(food)* vrhnje
  (for face etc) krema
credit card kreditna kartica
crew posada
crisps čips
Croatia Hrvatska
Croatian *(man)* Hrvat
  (woman) Hrvatica
  (adj, language) hrvatski
crowd gužva
cruise krstarenje
crutches štake
cry *(weep)* plakati
  (shout) vikati
cucumber krastavac
cufflink dugme za manšetu
cup šalica
cupboard ormar
curlers vikleri
curls kovrčava kosa
curry kari
curtain zavjesa
Customs carina

cut *(noun)* rez
  (verb) rezati

dad tata
dairy *(shop)* mljekara
Dalmatian *(adj)* dalmatinski
damp vlažno
dance ples
dangerous opasan
dark taman
daughter kćerka
day dan
dead mrtav
deaf gluh
dear *(person)* drag
  (expensive) skup
deckchair ležaljka
deep duboko
deliberately namjerno
dentist zubar
dentures umjetno zubalo
deny poreči
  I deny it ja to poričem
deodorant dezodorans
department store robna kuća
departure odlazak
develop *(a film)* razviti
diamond *(jewel)* dijamant
  (cards) karo
diarrhoea proljev
diary dnevnik
dictionary rječnik
die umrijeti
diesel dizel
different drukčiji
  that's different to je drukčije
  I'd like a different one molim vas nešto drugo
difficult teško

dining car vagon restoran
dining room blagavaonica
directory *(telephone)* telefonski imenik
dirty prljav
disabled invalid
distributor *(car)* razvodnik
dive roniti
diving board odskočna daska
divorced razveden
do činiti
doctor liječnik, doktor
document dokument
dog pas
doll lutka
dollar dolar
door vrata
double room soba s bračnim krevetom
doughnut krafna
down dolje
drawing pin čavlić
dress *(woman's)* haljina
drink *(verb)* piti
(noun) piće
would you like a drink? hoćete li nešto popiti?
drinking water pitka voda
drive *(verb)* voziti
driver vozač
driving licence vozačka dozvola
drunk pijan
dry suh
dry cleaner kemijska čistionica
dummy *(for baby)* duda
during za vrijeme
dustbin kanta za smeće
duster krpa za prašinu
Dutch holandski
duty-free duty-free

each *(every)* svaki
twenty dinars each po dvadeset dinara
early rano
earrings naušnice
ears uši
east istok
easy lagano
eat jesti
egg jaje
either: either of them ijedno
either ... or ... ili ... ili ...
elastic elastičan
elastic band guma lastika
elbow lakat
electric električan
electricity struja
else: something else nešto drugo
someone else netko drugi
somewhere else negdje drugdje
embarrassing nezgodno
embassy ambasada
embroidery vez
emerald smaragd
emergency hitan slučaj
emergency brake kočnica za opasnost
empty prazan
end *(noun)* kraj
(verb) završiti
engaged *(couple)* zaručnici
(occupied) zauzeto
engine *(motor)* motor
England Engleska
English engleski
(language) engleski
Englishman Englez
Englishwoman Engleskinja
enlargement povećanje
enough dosta
entertainment zabava

entrance ulaz
envelope koverat
escalator pomične stepenice
especially naročito
evening večer
every svako
everyone svaki, svi
everything sve
everywhere svugdje
example primjer
  for example na primjer
excellent odlično
excess baggage višak
  prtljage
exchange *(verb)* zamijeniti
exchange rate kurs
excursion izlet
excuse me! *(to get attention)*
  molim vas!
exit izlaz
expensive skup
extension produžetak
eye oko
eye drops kapljice za oči
eyes oči

face lice
faint *(unclear)* blijedo
  (verb) onesvijestiti se
  to feel faint osjećati se slabim
fair *(funfair)* luna park
  country fair vašar
  it's not fair to nije pravedno
false teeth umjetno zubalo
family porodica
fan *(ventilator)* ventilator
  (enthusiast) ljubimac
fan belt remen
far daleko

how far is ...? koliko je daleko
  do ...?
fare vozarina
farm farma
farmer farmer
fashion moda
fast brz
fat *(man)* debeo
  (woman) debela
  (on meat etc) masno
father otac
feel *(touch)* dodirnuti
  I feel hot vruće mi je
  I feel like ... želio bih ...
  I don't feel well ne osjećam se
  dobro
feet stopala
felt-tip pen flomaster ®
ferry trajekt
fever groznica
fiancé zaručnik
fiancée zaručnica
field polje
fig smokva
filling *(tooth)* plomba
  (sandwich etc) fila
film film
filter filter
finger prst
fire vatra
  (blaze) požar
fire extinguisher sprava za gašenje
  požara
fireworks vatromet
first prvi
first aid prva pomoć
first floor prvi kat
fish riba
fishing ribolov
  to go fishing ići u ribolov
fishing rod štap za pecanje
fishmonger ribarnica

fizzy gazirano
flag zastava
flash *(camera)* fleš
flat *(level)* ravan
  (apartment) stan
flavour okus
flea buha
flight let
flip-flops japanke
flippers peraje
flour brašno
flower cvijet
flu gripa
flute flauta
fly *(verb)* letjeti
  (insect) muha
fog magla
folk music folklorna muzika
  (Croatian also) folklorna glazba
food hrana
food poisoning otrovanje želuca
foot stopalo
football *(Croatian)* nogomet
  (Serbian) fudbal
  (ball) nogometna lopta
for za
  for me za mene
  what for? zašto?
  for a week na tjedan dana
foreigner stranac
forest šuma
fork viljuška
fortnight dva tjedna
fountain pen pero
fourth četvrti
fracture prijelom
France Francuska
free slobodan
  (no cost) besplatan
freezer zamrzivač
French *(adj, language)*
  francuski

Frenchman Francuz
Frenchwoman Francuskinja
fridge hladnjak
friend prijatelj
friendly prijateljski
front: in front of ... ispred ...
frost mraz
fruit voće
fruit juice voćni sok
fry pržiti
frying pan tava
full pun
  I'm full sit sam
full board puni pansion
funnel *(for pouring)* lijevak
funny smiješan
  (odd) čudan
furniture namještaj

garage garaža
garden vrt
garlic češnjak
gas-permeable lenses plinski
  propusne leće
gay *(homosexual)* homoseksualac
gear zupčanik
gear lever mjenjač
gents *(toilet)* muški
German *(man)* Nijemac
  (woman) Njemica
  (adj, language) njemački
Germany Njemačka
get *(fetch)* ići po
  have you got ...? imate li ...?
  to get the train uzeti vlak
get back: we get back tomorrow
  sutra se vraćamo
  to get something back dobiti
  nešto natrag

get in ući
  (arrive) stići
get out izići
get up *(rise)* ustati
gift poklon
gin džin
girl djevojka
girlfriend djevojka
give dati
glad sretan
  I'm glad sretan sam
glass staklo
  (to drink) čaša
glasses naočale
gloss prints fotografije na sjajnom papiru
gloves rukavice
glue ljepilo
go ići
  let's go idemo
  I'm going to Split idem u Split
goggles maska
gold zlato
good dobar
  good! dobro!
goodbye doviđenja
government vlada
granddaughter unuka
grandfather đed
grandmother baka
grandson unuk
grapes grožđe
grass trava
Great Britain Velika Britanija
Greece Grčka
Greek *(man)* Grk
  (woman) Grkinja
  (adj, language) grčki
Greek Orthodox pravoslavac
green zeleno
grey sivo
grill roštilj

grocer *(shop)* špeceraj
ground floor prizemlje
guarantee *(noun)* garancija
  (verb) osigurati
guard čuvar
guide book turistički vodič
guitar gitara
gun *(rifle)* puška
  (pistol) pištolj

hair kosa
haircut šišanje
hairdo frizura
hairdresser frizer
hair dryer fen
hair spray lak za kosu
half pola
  half an hour pola sata
half board polupansion
ham šunka
hamburger hamburger
hammer čekić
hand ruka
handbag tašna
hand brake ručna kočnica
handkerchief maramica
  (Croatian also) rupčić
handle *(door)* kvaka
handsome zgodan
hangover mamurluk
happy sretan
harbour luka
hard tvrd
  (difficult) teško
hard lenses krute leće
hat šešir
have imati
  I don't have ... nemam ...
  can I have ...? dajte mi ...?

have you got ...? imate li ...?
I have to go now moram ići
   sada
hayfever peludna groznica
he on
head glava
headache glavobolja
headlights farovi
hear čuti
hearing aid slušno pomagalo
heart srce
   (cards) herc
heart attack srčani udar
heating grijanje
heavy težak
heel peta
hello zdravo
help *(noun)* pomoć
   (verb) pomoći
   help! u pomoć!
her: it's her to je ona
   it's for her to je za nju
   give it to her dajte joj ga
   her book njena knjiga
   her child njeno dijete
   her hotel njen hotel
   her shoes njene cipele
   it's hers to je njeno
here ovdje
hi zdravo
high visoko
highway code prometni zakon
hill brdo
him: it's him to je on
   it's for him to je za njega
   give it to him dajte mu ga
hire iznajmiti
his: his book njegova knjiga
   his child njegovo dijete
   his hotel njegov hotel
   his shoes njegove cipele
   it's his to je njegovo

history povijest
hitch-hike autostopirati
hobby hobi
Holland Nizozemska, Holandija
holiday praznik
honest pošten
honey med
honeymoon medeni mjesec
horn *(car)* truba
   (animal) rog
horrible grozno
hospital bolnica
hour sat
house kuća
how? kako?
Hungarian *(man)* Mađar
   (woman) Mađarica
   (adj) mađarski
Hungary Mađarksa
hungry: I'm hungry ja sam
   gladan
hurry: I'm in a hurry žuri mi se
husband suprug, muž
hydrofoil hidrogliser

I ja
ice led
ice cream sladoled
ice cube kocka leda
ice lolly sladoled na štapiću
if ako
ignition paljenje
ill bolestan
immediately odmah
impossible nemoguće
in u
   in English na engleskom
   in the hotel u hotelu
India Indija

Indian *(man)* Indijac
  (woman) Indijka
  (adj) indijski
indicator pokazalo
indigestion loša probava
infection zaraza
information informacije
injection injekcija
injury ozljeda
ink tinta
inner tube unutarnja guma
insect insekt
insect repellent sredstvo protiv
  insekata
insomnia besanica
insurance osiguranje
interesting interesantno
interpret tumačiti
invitation poziv
Ireland Irska
Irish irski
Irishman Irac
Irishwoman Irkinja
iron *(metal)* željezo
  (for clothes) pegla
ironmonger željezarnica
is: he/she/it is ... on/ona/ono
  je ...
island *(Croatian)* otok
  (Serbian) ostrvo
it ono
  it's mine moje je
  it's in my room u mojoj je
  sobi
Italian *(man)* Talijan
  (woman) Talijanka
  (adj, language) talijanski
Italy Italija
itch *(noun)* svrbež
  it itches svrbi

jacket jakna
jam džem
jazz džez
jealous ljubomoran
jeans traperice
jellyfish meduza
jeweller zlatar
job posao
jog *(verb)* ići u jogging
  to go for a jog ići u jogging
joke šala
journey putovanje
jumper pulover
just: it's just arrived upravo je
  stiglo
  I've just one left samo mi je
  jedan ostao

key ključ
kidney bubreg
kilo kilogram
kilometre kilometar
kitchen kuhinja
knee koljeno
knife nož
knit plesti
know: I don't know ne znam

label etiketa
lace čipka
laces *(of shoe)* žniranci
ladies *(toilet)* ženski
lake jezero
lamb janje

lamp lampa
lampshade sjenilo
land *(noun)* zemlja
  (verb) sletjeti
language jezik
large velik
last *(final)* posljednji
  last week/month prošli tjedan/
  mjesec
  at last! konačno!
late: it's getting late već je kasno
  the bus is late autobus kasni
laugh smijeh
laundry *(place)* praonica
  (dirty clothes) prljavo rublje
laxative laksativ
lazy lijen
leaf list
leaflet letak
learn učiti
leather koža
left *(not right)* lijevo
  there's nothing left nema više
  ništa
left luggage *(locker)* garderoba
leg noga
lemon limun
lemonade limunada
length dužina
lens leće
less manje
lesson sat
letter pismo
letterbox poštanski sanduk
lettuce zelena salata
library knjižnica
licence dozvola
life život
lift *(in building)* lift
  (Croatian also) dizalo
  could you give me a lift?
  možete li me prebaciti?

light *(not heavy)* lagan
  (not dark) svijetlo
lighter upaljač
lighter fuel gorivo za upaljač
light meter svjetlomjer
like: I like you sviđaš mi se
  I like swimming volim plivati
  it's like ... to je poput ...
lip salve mast za usne
lipstick ruž za usne
liqueur liker
list spisak
litre litra
litter smeće
little *(small)* mali
  it's a little big malo je preveliko
  just a little samo malo
liver jetra
lobster jastog
lollipop lilihip
long dugo
  how long does it take? koliko
  dugo traje?
lorry kamion
lost property izgubljeno-nađeno
  I'm lost izgubio sam se
lot: a lot puno
loud glasno
  (colour) kričav
lounge salon
love *(noun)* ljubav
  (verb) voljeti
lover *(man)* ljubavnik
  (woman) ljubavnica
low nisko
luck sreća
  good luck! sretno!
luggage prtljaga
luggage rack polica za prtljagu
lunch ručak

magazine časopis
mail pošta
make napraviti
make-up šminka
man čovjek
manager rukovodilac
map *(of city)* plan grada
   (of country) mapa zemlje
   a map of Belgrade plan grada
   Beograda
marble mramor
margarine margarin
market tržnica
marmalade marmelada od
   naranči
married *(man)* oženjen
   (woman) udata
mascara maskara
mass *(church)* misa
mast jarbol
match *(light)* šibica
   (sport) utakmica
material *(cloth)* štof
mattress madrac
maybe možda
me: it's me ja sam
   it's for me to je za mene
   give it to me dajte mi ga
meal obrok
meat meso
mechanic mehaničar
medicine lijek
meeting sastanak
melon dinja
menu jelovnik
message poruka
midday podne
middle: in the middle u sredini
midnight ponoć
milk mlijeko
mine: it's mine to je moje

mineral water mineralna voda
minute minuta
mirror ogledalo
Miss gospođica
mistake greška
   to make a mistake pogriješiti
monastery manastir
money novac
month mjesec
monument spomenik
moon mjesec
moped moped
more još
morning jutro
   in the morning ujutro
mosaic mozaik
mosquito komarac
mother majka
motorbike motocikl
motorboat motorni čamac
motorway autoput
mountain planina
mouse miš
moustache brkovi
mouth usta
move pokret
   don't move! ne miči se!
   (house) preseliti se
movie film
Mr gospodin
Mrs gospođa
much: not much ne puno
   much better/slower puno bolje/
   sporije
mug šalica
   a mug of coffee šalica kave
mule mazga
mum mama
museum muzej
mushroom gljiva
music muzika
   (Croatian also) glazba

musical instrument *(Croatian)*
  glazbalo
  (Serbian) muzički instrument
musician muzičar
mussels dagnje
mustard senf
my: my bag moja tašna
  my egg moje jaje
  my swimsuit moj kupači
  kostim
  my keys moji ključevi
mythology mitologija

nail *(metal)* čavao
  (finger) nokat
nail file turpija
nail polish lak za nokte
name ime
nappy pelena
narrow uzak
near: near the door blizu vrata
  near London blizu Londona
necessary potrebno
necklace ogrlica
need *(verb)* trebati
  I need ... trebam ...
  there's no need ne treba
needle igla
negative *(photo)* negativ
neither: neither of them
  nijedan od njih
neither ... nor ... niti ... niti ...
nephew nečak
never nikada
new nov
news novosti
newsagent prodavač novina
newspaper novine
New Zealand Novi Zeland

New Zealander *(man)*
  Novozelanđanin
  (woman) Novozelanđanka
next slijedeći
  next week/month slijedeći
  tjedan/mjesec
  what next? što sad?
nice lijepo
niece nečakinja
night noć
nightclub noćni lokal
nightdress spavaćica
night porter noćni portir
no *(response)* ne
  I have no money nemam novaca
  there are no towels nema rućnika
noisy bučan
north sjever
Northern Ireland Sjeverna Irska
nose nos
not ne
notebook bilježnica
nothing ništa
novel roman
now sada
nowhere nigdje
nudist nudist
nudist beach nudističa plaža
number broj
number plate registarska ploča
nurse medicinska sestra
nut *(for bolt)* matica

occasionally povremeno
octopus hobotnica
of od
office kancelarija
often često
oil ulje

ointment mast
OK OK
old star
olive maslina
omelette omlet
on na
one jedan
onion luk
only samo
open *(verb)* otvoriti
  (adj) otvoren
opposite: opposite the hotel
  nasuprot hotela
optician optičar
or ili
orange *(colour)* narančasta boja
  (fruit) naranča
orange juice sok od naranče
orchestra orkestar
ordinary *(normal)* uobičajeno
organ organ
  (music) orgulje
our naš
  it's ours to je naše
out: he's out on je vani
outside vani
over preko
  over there tamo
overtake pretjecati
oyster oštriga

pack of cards špil karata
package paket
packet paket
  a packet of ... paket ...
padlock katanac
page stranica
pain bol
paint *(noun)* boja

pair par
Pakistan Pakistan
Pakistani *(man)* Pakistanac
  (woman) Pakistanka
  (adj) pakistanski
pale blijed
pancakes palačinke
paper papir
parcel paket
pardon? molim?
parents roditelji
park *(noun)* park
  (verb) parkirati se
parsley peršun
party *(celebration)* zabava
  (group) grupa
  (political) partija
passenger putnik
passport pasoš
pasta tjestenina
path puteljak
pavement pločnik
pay platiti
peach breskva
peanuts kikiriki
pear kruška
pearl biser
peas grašak
pedestrian pješak
peg *(for clothes)* štipaljka
pen pero
pencil olovka
pencil sharpener šiljilo
penfriend prijatelj putem dopisivanja
peninsula poluotok
penknife džepni nož
people ljudi
pepper *(& salt)* biber
  (red/green) paprika
peppermints pepermint
per: per person po osobi
perfect savršeno

perfume parfem
perhaps možda
perm trajna
petrol benzin
petrol station benzinska stanica
petticoat potkošulja
photograph *(noun)* fotografija
  (verb) slikati
photographer fotograf
phrase book turistički rječnik
piano klavir
pickpocket džeparoš
picnic piknik
piece komad
pillow jastuk
pilot pilot
pin igla
pine *(tree)* jelka
pineapple ananas
pink ružičasta boja
pipe *(for smoking)* lula
  (for water) cijev
piston stap
pizza pizza
place mjesto
plant biljka
plaster *(for cut)* flaster
plastic plastika
plastic bag plastična vrečica
plate tanjur
platform tribina
play *(theatre)* kazališni komad
please molim
plug *(electrical)* utičnica
  (sink) čep
pocket džep
poison otrov
police milicija
policeman milicajac
police station milicijska stanica
politics politika
poor siromašan

(bad quality) loš
pop music pop muzika
  (Croatian also) pop glazba
pork svinjetina
port *(harbour)* luka
porter *(for luggage)* nosač
  (hotel) portir
possible moguće
post *(noun)* pošta
  (verb) poslati poštom
post box poštanski sanduk
postcard razglednica
poster plakat
postman poštar
post office pošta
potato krumpir
poultry živad
pound *(money, weight)* funta
powder *(for face, baby)* puder
pram dječja kolica
prawn morski račić
prescription recept
pretty *(beautiful)* lijep
  (quite) prilično
priest svečenik
private privatno
problem problem
  what's the problem? u čemu je
  problem?
protection factor zaštitni faktor
public publika
  (adj) javni
pull vuci
puncture probušena guma
purple ljubičasta boja
purse novčanik
push rini
pushchair dječja kolica
pyjamas pidžame

quality kvaliteta
quay molo
question pitanje
queue *(noun)* rep
  (verb) stati u rep
quick brz
quiet tih
quite *(fairly)* prilično
  (fully) potpuno

radiator radijator
radio radio
radish rotkvica
railway line željeznička pruga
rain kiša
raincoat kišna kabanica
raisins grožđice
rare *(uncommon)* rijedak
  (steak) krvavo
rat štakor
razor blades žilet ®
read čitati
reading lamp stolna lampa
  (bed) lampa pokraj kreveta
ready spremno
rear lights poziciona svjetla
receipt račun
receptionist recepcionist
record *(music)* gramofonska ploča
  (sporting etc) rekord
record player gramofon
record shop prodavaonica
  gramofonskih ploča
red crven
red wine crno vino
refreshments laki obroci
registered letter preporučeno
  pismo
relative rođak

relax opustiti se
religion vjera
remember sjetiti se
  I don't remember ne sjećam se
rent *(verb)* iznajmiti
reservation rezervacija
rest *(remainder)* ostatak
  (relax) odmarati se
restaurant restoran
restaurant car vagon restoran
return *(come back)* vratiti se
  (give back) vratiti
return ticket povratna karta
rice riža
rich bogat
right *(correct)* točno
  (direction) desno
ring *(to call)* nazvati
  (wedding etc) prsten
ripe zreo
river rijeka
road cesta
rock *(stone)* kamen
  (music) rock muzika
  (Croatian) rock glazba
roll *(bread)* žemlja
Romania Rumunjska
Romanian *(man)* Rumunj
  (woman) Rumunjka
  (adj) rumunjski
roof krov
room soba
  (space) mjesto
rope uže
rose ruža
round *(circular)* okrugao
  it's my round ja častim
rowing boat čamac
rubber *(eraser)* gumica
  (material) guma
rubbish smeće
ruby *(stone)* rubin

rucksack ruksak
rug *(mat)* sag
  (blanket) pokrivač
ruins ruševine
ruler *(for drawing)* ravnalo
rum rum
run *(person)* trčati
runway pista

sad tužan
safe siguran
safety pin ziherica
sailing boat jedrilica
salad salata
salami salama
sale *(at reduced prices)*
  rasprodaja
salmon losos
salt sol
same: the same dress ista
  haljina
  the same people isti ljudi
  same again please još jedno
  molim
sand pijesak
sandals sandale
sand dunes pješčane dine
sandwich sendvič
sanitary towels higijenski ulošci
sauce umak
saucepan lonac
sauna sauna
sausage kobasica
say reći
  what did you say? što kažete?
  how do you say ...? kako se
  kaže ...?
scarf šal
  (head) marama

school škola
scissors škare
Scottish škotski
Scotland Škotska
screw šaraf
screwdriver odvijač
sea more
seafood morski specijaliteti
seat sjedalo
seat belt sigurnosni pojas
second *(of time)* sekunda
  (in series) drugi
see vidjeti
  I can't see ne vidim
  I see *(understand)* razumijem
sell prodati
sellotape ® selotejp
separate razdvojiti
separated razdvojeni
Serbia Srbija
Serbian *(adj, language)* srpski
Serbocroat srpskohrvatski
serious ozbiljan
serviette salveta
several nekoliko
sew šiti
shampoo šampon
shave *(noun)* brijanje
  (verb) obrijati se
shaving foam pjena za brijanje
shawl šal
she ona
sheet plahta
shell školjka
ship brod
shirt košulja
shoe laces žniranci
shoe polish laštilo za cipele
shoes cipele
shop prodavaonica
shopping kupovina
  to go shopping ići u kupovinu

short kratak
  (person) nizak
shorts kratke hlače
shoulder rame
shower *(bath)* tuš
  (rain) pljusak
shrimp račić
shutter *(camera)* blenda
  (window) žaluzine
sick *(ill)* bolestan
  I feel sick bolestan sam
side *(edge)* rub
  I'm on her side ja sam na
  njenoj strani
sidelights poziciona svjetla
sights: the sights of ... povjesni
  i kulturni spomenici ...
silk svila
silver *(colour)* srebrna boja
  (metal) srebro
simple jednostavno
sing pjevati
single *(one)* jedan jedini
  (unmarried) samac
single room jednokrevetna soba
sister sestra
skid *(verb)* skliznuti
skin cleanser mlijeko za čišćenje
  lica
skirt suknja
sky nebo
sleep *(noun)* san
  (verb) spavati
  to go to sleep zaspati
sleeping bag vreća za spavanje
sleeping pill sredstvo za spavanje
slippers papuče
slivovitz šljivovica
slow spor
small mali
smell *(noun)* miris
  (verb) mirisati

smile *(noun)* osmjeh
  (verb) smiješiti se
smoke *(noun)* dim
  (verb) pušiti
snack laki obrok
snorkel disaljka *(za ronjenje)*
snow snijeg
so: so good tako dobro
  not so much ne toliko
soaking solution *(for contact
  lenses)* tekućina za kontaktne leće
socks čarape
soda water soda
soft lenses mekane leće
somebody netko
somehow nekako
something nešto
sometimes ponekad
somewhere negdje
son sin
song pjesma
sorry! oprostite!
  I'm sorry žao mi je
soup juha
south jug
South Africa Južna Afrika
South African *(man)*
  Južnoafrikanac
  (woman) Južnoafrikanka
  (adj) južnoafrički
souvenir suvenir
spade *(shovel)* lopata
  (cards) pik
spanner ključ za odvijanje
spares rezervni djelovi
spark(ing) plug svjećica
speak govoriti
  do you speak ...? govorite li ...?
  I don't speak ... ne govorim ...
speed brzina
speed limit ograničena brzina
speedometer brzinomjer

spider pauk
spinach špinat
spoon žlica
sprain zavrnuti
spring *(mechanical)* opruga
  (season) proljeće
stadium stadion
staircase stepenište
stairs stepenice
stamp marka
stapler klamerica
star *(in sky, film)* zvijezda
start *(verb)* početi
station *(Croatian)* kolodvor
  (Serbian) stanica
statue kip
steak biftek
steal krasti
  it's been stolen ukradeno je
steering wheel volan
stewardess stjuardesa
sting *(noun)* ubod
  (verb) ubosti
  it stings peče
stockings čarape
stomach želudac
stomach ache bol u želucu
stop *(verb)* stati
  (bus stop) stajalište autobusa
  stop! stoj!
storm oluja
strawberry jagoda
stream *(small river)* potok
street ulica
string *(cord)* špaga
  (guitar etc) žica
student student
stupid blesav
suburbs predgrađe
sugar šećer
suit *(noun)* odijelo
  (verb) odgovarati

it suits you *(formal)* dobro vam
  stoji
  (familiar) dobro ti stoji
suitcase kofer
sun sunce
sunbathe sunčati se
sunburn opaljenost od sunca
sunglasses sunčane naočale
sunny: it's sunny sunčan je dan
suntan: to get a suntan pocrnjeti
  od sunca
suntan lotion losion za sunčanje
supermarket samoposluga
supplement doplata
sure siguran
  are you sure? jeste li sigurni?
surname prezime
sweat *(noun)* znoj
  (verb) znojiti se
sweatshirt majica
sweet *(not sour)* slatko
  (candy) slatkiši
swimming costume kupaći kostim
swimming pool bazen
swimming trunks kupaće gaćice
Swiss *(man)* Švicarac
  (woman) Švicarka
  (adj) švicarski
switch gumb
Switzerland Švicarska
synagogue sinagog

table stol
tablet tableta
take uzeti
take away: to take away za van
take off *(noun)* uzletanje
  (verb) uzletjeti
talcum powder talk

talk *(noun)* govor
  (verb) govoriti
tall visok
tampon tampon
tangerine mandarinka
tap slavina
tapestry tapiserija
tea čaj
tea towel kuhinjska krpa
telegram telegram
  (Croatian also) brzojav
telephone *(noun)* telefon
  (verb) telefonirati
telephone box telefonska
  govornica
telephone call telefonski poziv
television televizija
temperature temperatura
tent šator
tent peg šatorski kalčić
tent pole šatorska motka
than nego
thank *(verb)* zahvaliti se
  thanks hvala
  thank you hvala vam
that: that bus/man taj autobus/
  čovjek
  that quay to molo
  that woman ta žena
  what's that? što je to?
  I think that ... mislim da ...
their: their room njihova soba
  their books njihove knjige
  it's theirs to je njihovo
them: it's them to su oni
  it's for them to je za njih
  give it to them dajte im ga
then onda
there tamo
  there is/are ... ima ...
  is/are there ...? ima li ...?
thermos flask termosica

these: these things ove stvari
  these are mine ove su moje
they oni
thick debelo
thin tanko
think misliti
  I think so ja tako mislim
  I'll think about it razmislit ću
third treći
thirsty: I'm thirsty ja sam žedan
this: this bus/man ovaj autobus/
  čovjek
  this woman ova žena
  what's this? što je ovo?
  this is Mr ... ovo je gospodin ...
those: those things te stvari
  those are his te su njegove
throat grlo
throat pastilles septolete ®
through kroz
thunderstorm grmljevina
ticket karta
tie *(noun)* kravata
  (verb) zavezati
tights hulahopke
time vrijeme
  what's the time? koliko je sati?
timetable raspored
tin limenka
tin opener otvarač za limenke
tip *(money)* napojnica
  (end) vrh
tired umoran
  I feel tired umoran sam
tissues papirnate maramice
to: to England u Englesku
  to the station na kolodvor
  to the doctor kod liječnika
toast tost
tobacco duhan
today danas
together zajedno

toilet toalet
toilet paper toaletni papir
tomato *(Croatian)* rajčica
 (Serbian) paradajz
tomato juice sok od rajčica/
 paradajza
tomorrow sutra
tongue jezik
tonic tonik
tonight večeras
too *(also)* također
 (excessive) previše
tooth zub
toothache zubobolja
toothbrush četka za zube
toothpaste pasta za zube
topless toples
torch baterija
tour razgledavanje
tourist turist
tourist office turistički biro
towel ručnik
tower kula
town grad
town hall viječnica
toy igračka
toy shop prodavaonica igračaka
track suit trenirka
tractor traktor
tradition tradicija
traffic promet
traffic jam zastoj u prometu
traffic lights semafori
trailer *(behind car)* prikolica
train *(Croatian)* vlak
 (Serbian) voz
translate prevesti
transmission *(for car)* transmisija
travel agency turistička agencija
traveller's cheque putnički ček
tray tacna
tree stablo

trousers hlače
try pokušati
tunnel tunel
Turkey Turska
tweezers pinceta
typewriter pisaći stroj
tyre guma

umbrella kišobran
uncle ujak
under ispod
underground podzemna željeznica
underpants gaće
understand razumjeti
 I don't understand ne razumijem
underwear donje rublje
university *(Croatian)* sveučilište
 (Serbian) univerzitet
unmarried *(man)* neoženjen
 (woman) neudata
until do
unusual neobičan
up: up there tamo gore
 further up još gore
 he's not up nije još ustao
urgent hitno
us: it's us mi smo
 it's for us to je za nas
 give it to us dajte nam ga
use *(noun)* upotreba
 (verb) upotrijebiti
 it's no use ne vrijedi
useful korisno
usual običan
usually obično

vacancy *(room)* slobodna soba
vacuum cleaner usisivač
vacuum flask termosica
valley dolina
valve ventil
vanilla vanilija
vase vaza
veal teletina
vegetable povrće
vegetarian *(person)* vegetarijanac
vehicle vozilo
very vrlo
  thank you very much puno hvala
  I like it very much puno mi se sviđa
vest potkošulja
view pogled
viewfinder tražilo
villa vila
village selo
vinegar ocat
violin violina
visa viza
visit *(noun)* posjeta
  (verb) posjetiti
visitor posjetilac
  (tourist) turist
vitamin tablet vitamini
vodka votka
voice glas

wait čekati
waiter konobar
  waiter! konobar!
waiting room čekaonica
waitress konobarica
  waitress! konobarice!
Wales Wales

walk *(noun: stroll)* šetnja
  (verb) šetati
  to go for a walk ići u šetnju
walkman ® walkman
wall zid
wallet novčanik
war rat
wardrobe ormar
warm toplo
was: I was *(man)* bio sam
  (woman) bila sam
  he was on je bio
  she was ona je bila
  it was bilo je
washing powder prašak za pranje rublja
washing-up liquid tekućina za pranje suđa
wasp osa
watch *(noun)* ručni sat
  (verb) posmatrati
water voda
waterfall vodopad
wave *(noun)* val
  (verb) mahati
we mi
weather vrijeme
wedding svadba
week tjedan
welcome dobrodošli
  you're welcome *(don't mention it)* molim, nema na če mu
wellingtons gumene čizme
Welsh velški
were: we were mi smo bili
  you were vi ste bili
  (sing. familiar) (man) ti si bio
  (woman) ti si bila
  they were oni su bili
west zapad
wet mokar
what? što?

wheel kotač
wheelchair invalidska kolica
when? kada?
where? gdje?
whether da li
which? koji?
whisky viski
white bijelo
white wine bijelo vino
who? tko?
why? zašto?
wide široko
wife supruga, žena
wind vjetar
window prozor
windscreen prednje staklo
wine vino
wine list cjenik vina
wing krilo
with sa
without bez
woman žena
wood drvo
wool vuna
word riječ
work *(noun)* rad
   (verb) raditi
worse gore
worst najgore
wrapping paper papir za
   omotavanje
   (for presents) poklon papir
wrist ručni zglob
writing paper papir za pisanje
   pisma
wrong krivo

year godina
yellow žuta boja
yes da
yesterday jučer
yet još
   not yet ne još
yoghurt jogurt
you vi
   (sing. familiar) ti
   for you *(familiar)* za tebe
   (polite) za vas
   with you *(familiar)* s tobom
   (polite) s vama
your: your book *(familiar)* tvoja
   knjiga
   (polite) vaša knjiga
   your child *(familiar)* tvoje dijete
   (polite) vaše dijete
   your hotel *(familiar)* tvoj hotel
   (polite) vaš hotel
   your shoes *(familiar)* tvoje cipele
   (polite) vaše cipele
yours: is this yours? *(familiar)* da
   i je ovo tvoje?
   (polite) da li je ovo vaše?
youth hostel omladinski hotel
Yugoslav *(man)* Jugoslaven
   (woman) Jugoslavenka
   (adj) jugoslavenski
Yugoslavia Jugoslavija

zip patent zatvarač
zoo zoološki vrt